Action at the Grassroots: Fighting Poverty and Environmental Decline

Alan B. Durning

Worldwatch Paper 88
January 1989

Sections of this paper may be reproduced in magazines and newspapers with acknowledgment to the Worldwatch Institute. The views expressed in this paper are those of the author and do not necessarily represent those of the Worldwatch Institute and its directors, officers, or staff, or of funding organizations.

Library of Congress Catalog Card Number 88-51968
ISBN 0-916468-89-5

Printed on Recycled Paper

Table of Contents

Introduction 5

Rising Grassroots Movements 8

The Genesis of Local Action 17

Meeting Human Needs 22

Earning Our Daily Bread .28

Protecting the Local Environment 32

Reforming Development Assistance 42

From the Bottom and the Top 50

Notes 56

Introduction

Women on the banks of the Ganges may not be able to calculate an infant mortality rate, but they know all too well the helplessness and agony of holding a child as it dies of diarrhea. Residents along the lower reaches of the Mississippi may not be able to name the mutagens and carcinogens that nearby petrochemical factories pump into their air and water, but they know how many of their neighbors have miscarried or died of cancer. Forest dwellers in the Amazon basin cannot quantify the mass extinction of species now occurring around them, but they know what it is to watch their primeval homeland go up in smoke before advancing waves of migrants and developers.

These people understand global degradation in its rawest forms. To them, creeping destruction of ecosystems has meant lengthening workdays, failing livelihoods, and deteriorating health. And it has pushed many of them to act. In villages, neighborhoods, and shantytowns around the world, people are coming together to strike back at the forces of environmental and economic decline that endanger our communities and our planet.

The global threat is complex and manifold. Each year, more babies are added to the world's population than ever before, primarily in the poorest nations. The pressure to feed the growing number of people helps cause rates of topsoil loss unprecedented since the dawn of agriculture. An area the size of Switzerland—6 million hectares—

The author would like to thank Susan Norris for production assistance, Sheldon Annis, David Beckmann, Medea Benjamin, Laurie Greenberg, Kevin Healy, Doug Hellinger, Larry Minear, Lloyd Timberlake, and Edward Wolf for comments on drafts of this paper, and the many people in Latin America who assisted in field research during 1988 for their generosity.

of productive land becomes desert each year. Because of increased population and decreased agricultural productivity, per capita grain yields have been declining in Africa since 1967 and in Latin America since 1981. Tropical forest habitat is being cleared so rapidly that one-fifth of the earth's species may be extinct by early in the next century. As the poorest nations struggle with these problems, some 17 million of their children die of preventable diseases annually. Meanwhile, increasing industrialization has produced acid rain and air pollution, causing the slow death of thousands of lakes, streams, and forests in northern latitudes and endangering human health. Most ominously, the entire planet's temperature appears to be rising, as heat-trapping gases released by industrial processes and deforestation accumulate in the atmosphere.[1]

In the face of such enormous threats, isolated grassroots initiatives appear minuscule—10 women plant trees on a roadside, a local union strikes for a nontoxic work place, an old man teaches neighborhood children to read—but, when added together, their impact has the potential to reshape the earth. Those who live economic and environmental decline are not only the most cognizant of the perils facing our planet, they are the ragtag front line in the worldwide struggle to end poverty and environmental destruction.

Although most groups are little known beyond provincial borders, the outlines of an overall movement emerge by piecing together insights from scores of interviews, field visits, grassroots newsletters, official documents, press reports, and academic papers. The picture shows an expanding latticework covering the globe. Viewed closely, these groups vary enormously in most particulars but share many fundamental characteristics.[2]

The particulars include cooperatives, mothers clubs, suburban groundwater committees, peasant farming unions, religious study groups, neighborhood action federations, collective aid societies, tribal nations, and innumerable others. The shared characteristics include the capacities to tap local knowledge and resources, to respond to problems rapidly and creatively, and to maintain the flexibility needed

"The world's people are better organized in 1989 than they have been since European colonialism disrupted traditional societies centuries ago."

in changing circumstances. In addition, although few groups use the term sustainable development, their agendas often embody this ideal. They want economic prosperity without sacrificing their health or the prospects for their children.

At the local level, particularly among the close to 4 billion humans in developing lands, it appears that the world's people are better organized in 1989 than they have been since European colonialism disrupted traditional societies centuries ago. Alone, this new class of organizations is far from powerful enough to set the world on a sustainable course. The work required—from slowing excessive population growth to reforesting the planet's denuded watersheds—will involve an unprecedented outpouring of human energy. The tasks are far from mysterious; in fact, millions have been engaged in them for years. But achieving a just and sustainable global economy will require an enormous number of simple acts.

Grassroots groups, whose membership now numbers in the hundreds of millions, may be able to show the world how to tap the energy to perform these acts. In turn, national governments and international agencies, which have all too often excluded or sought to control popular organizations, must learn to work with them. Forming an equal partnership between local organizations and government bodies built on mutual respect and shared goals seems a prerequisite to resolving many of the tenacious problems confronting the planet. Development institutions, for their part, will need to dramatically decentralize their decision making and integrate new participatory methods into their operations if they are to fulfill their potential as supporters of and complements to local efforts.[3]

The difficulty in forging an alliance between powerful, often rigid institutions and the world's millions of enthusiastic but fragile community action groups can scarcely be underestimated, yet neither can its importance. To succeed, sustainable development will have to come from both the bottom and the top.

8 Rising Grassroots Movements

Grassroots action is on the rise everywhere from Eastern Europe's industrial heartland, where fledgling environmental movements are demanding that human health no longer be sacrificed for economic growth, to the Himalayan foothills, where multitudes of Indian villagers are organized to protect and reforest barren slopes. As environmental decay accelerates in industrial regions, communities are organizing in growing numbers to protect themselves from chemical wastes, industrial pollution, and nuclear power installations. In developing countries, meanwhile, deepening poverty combined with often catastrophic ecological degradation has led to the proliferation of grassroots self-help movements. Whether based in the predominantly industrial North or developing South, these movements have begun to interlock as they find their common interests.

In the Third World, the birth of modern grassroots movements is a dramatic departure from historical precedents. In an anthropological sense, social organization is ubiquitous. Kinship, peer relations, division of labor, social hierarchies, and religious structures form the scaffolding of human community in traditional societies all over the world. Yet traditional tribal, village, and religious organizations, first disturbed by European colonialism, have been stretched and often dismantled by the great cultural upheavals of the twentieth century: rapid population growth, urbanization, the advent of modern technology, and the spread of western commercialism.[4]

In the resulting organizational vacuum, a new generation of community and grassroots groups has been steadily, albeit unevenly, developing since mid-century, and particularly over the past two decades. This evolution is driven by a shifting constellation of forces, including stagnant or deteriorating economic and environmental conditions for the poor, the failure of governments to respond to basic needs, the spread in some regions of new social ideologies and religious doctrines, and the political space opened in some countries as tight-

"This rising tide of community groups is generally pragmatic, focused on development, and concerned above all else with self-help."

fisted dictatorships give way to nascent democracies. In contrast to traditional organizations and mass political movements, this rising tide of community groups is generally pragmatic, focused on development, and concerned above all with self-help.

At the same time, a second layer of institutions has formed atop the grassroots layer in much of the Third World. This diverse class of intermediary organizations goes by many names: in Europe they are called nongovernmental organizations (NGOs), in the United States private voluntary organizations (PVOs), and in Asia voluntary agencies (or "Volags"). Here they will be called "independent development organizations" or simply "independent groups." Their general function is to facilitate the flow of information, materials, and funds between the grassroots and broader institutions such as church, state, and development donors. To do so, they tend to specialize—in appropriate technologies, for example, or in training for cooperatives—and to join informal federations of independent groups. The result in many countries is an intricate matrix of organizations catering to the grassroots.[5]

Numbers only crudely capture the vitality of the developing world's grassroots movements, since data are sketchy and groups fluid, yet the steady growth is unmistakable. Although at mid-century community development projects existed mainly where traditional self-help customs remained intact, today dynamic local organizations are found in many parts of the world. (See Table 1.)[6]

By many accounts, Asia has the most active communities. India's self-help movement has a prized place in society, tracing its roots to Mahatma Gandhi's pioneering village development work sixty years ago. Gandhi aimed to build a just and humane society from the bottom up, starting with self-reliant villages based on renewable resources. After independence in 1948, Gandhi's disciple Vinoba Bhave sparked the influential Village Awakening movement and, when that peaked in 1964, a new wave of community organizing commenced, spurred by a generation of committed middle-class youths. Tens if

Table 1: Grassroots Organizations in Selected Developing Countries, Late Eighties

Country	Description
Bangladesh	1,200 independent development organizations formed since 1971, particularly active in health and income generation with large landless population.
Brazil	Enormous growth in community action since democratization in early eighties: 100,000 Christian Base Communities with 3 million members; 1,300 neighborhood associations in São Paulo; landless peasant groups proliferating; 1,041 independent development organizations.
Burkina Faso	Naam grassroots peasant movement has 2,500 groups participating in dry-season self-help; similar movements forming in Senegal, Mauritania, Mali, Niger, and Togo.
India	Strong Gandhian self-help tradition promotes social welfare, appropriate technology, and tree planting; local groups number in at least the tens of thousands, independent development organizations estimated at 12,000.
Indonesia	600 independent development groups work in environmental protection alone; peasant irrigation groups multiplying.
Kenya	16,232 women's groups with 637,000 members registered in 1984, quadruple the 1980 number (1988 estimates range up to 25,000); many start as savings clubs.
Mexico	Massive urban grassroots movement active in squatter settlements of major cities; at least 250 independent development organizations.
Peru	Vital women's self-help movement in Lima's impoverished shantytowns, with 1,500 community kitchens; 300 independent development organizations.
Philippines	3,000–5,000 Christian Base Communities form focal points for local action.
Sri Lanka	Rapidly growing Sarvodaya Shramadana village awakening movement includes over 8,000 villages, one-third of total in country; 3 million people involved in range of efforts, particularly work parties, education, preventive health care, and cooperative crafts projects.
Zimbabwe	Small-farmer groups throughout country have estimated membership of 400,000, 80 percent women; active women's community gardens multiplying.

Source: Worldwatch Institute, based on numerous sources.

not hundreds of thousands of local groups in India now wage the day-by-day struggle for development.[7]

Across the subcontinent, community activism runs high. Self-help in Bangladesh has risen steadily since independence in 1971, and 3 million Sri Lankans participate in Sarvodaya Shramadana, a community-development movement that combines Gandhian teachings with social action tenets of Buddhism. Sarvodaya mobilizes massive work teams to do everything from building roads to draining malarial ponds.[8]

After Asia, Latin American communities appear to be the most active. The bulk of the continent's experience with local initiatives dates to the 1968 conference of Catholic Bishops in Medellín, Colombia, where the church fundamentally reoriented its social mission, toward improving the lot of the poor. Since that time, millions of priests, nuns, and laypersons have fanned out into the back streets and hinterlands from Tierra del Fuego to the Rio Grande, dedicating themselves to creating a people's church embodied in neighborhood worship and action groups called Christian Base Communities. Brazil alone has 100,000 of these organizations, with at least 3 million members, and an equal number are spread across the rest of the continent. In Central America, they play an important role in movements for peace and human rights.[9]

In Latin America, past political movements also laid the groundwork for current community self-help efforts. A decade ago, the rise and subsequent repression of Colombia's National Association of Small Farmers gave peasants experience with organizing that led to the abundance of community efforts today, including cooperative stores and environmental "green councils." In Nicaragua, the national uprising that overthrew the dictatorship of Anastasio Somoza in 1979 created a surge of grassroots energy that flowed into thousands of new cooperatives, women's groups, and community-development projects.[10]

Self-help organizations are relative newcomers to Africa, though traditional village institutions are stronger than in other regions. Nevertheless, in parts of Africa where political struggles have led to dramatic changes in political structures, local initiatives have sprung up in abundance. In Kenya, the harambee (let's pull together) movement began with independence in 1963 and, with encouragement from the national government, by the early eighties was contributing nearly one-third of all labor, materials, and finances invested in rural development. With Zimbabwe's transfer to black rule in 1980, a similar explosion in community organizing began, as thousands of women's community gardens and informal small-farmer associations formed. Senegal and Burkina Faso too are well organized at the grassroots level, as a result of traditions of village communal work.[11]

A noteworthy characteristic of community movements throughout the Third World is the central role that women play. In Africa the sheer enormity of women's burdens unites them: women bear primary responsibility for child care, cooking, cleaning, processing food, carrying water, and gathering fuel; they grow 80 percent of the food, raise half the livestock, and give birth to 27 million babies a year. Worldwide, women's traditional nurturing role may give them increased concern for the generations of their children and grandchildren, while their subordinate social status gives them more to gain from organizing.[12]

Unfortunately, the map of Third World local action has several blank spaces. Independent community-level organizations concentrating on self-help are scarce or non-existent in the Middle East, China, north Africa, large patches of sub-Saharan Africa, and northeastern India. Likewise, remote regions in many countries lack grassroots groups. Some of these absences are a result of cultural, religious, or political factors, as in China, where state-sanctioned local groups monopolize grassroots development. Northeastern India and sub-Saharan Africa, by contrast, are home to some of the poorest people on earth. The absence of local groups there may reflect a degree of misery that precludes expending energy on anything beyond survival.

"**The map of Third World local action has several blank spaces.**"

Outside the Third World, grassroots movements are also on the rise. In industrial nations of both East and West their concerns increasingly align them with the goal of creating sustainable societies. In the Soviet Union and Eastern Europe, where officially sanctioned local organizations are numerous but largely controlled by state and party hierarchies, the political openness of this decade has brought the genesis, often at considerable risk to the founders, of independent citizens groups. In addition to the Eastern bloc's internationally known labor movements and human rights organizations there are scores of local groups opposing nuclear power reactors and industrial polluters.[13]

Indeed, the East could be the environmental boom field of the nineties. Human rights monitors Brian Morton and Joanne Landy report: "During the period of *glasnost,* independent citizens' initiatives have sprung up in the Soviet Union 'like mushrooms after a rain,' as a Russian saying has it." Hundreds of independent and semi-independent ecology clubs have coalesced. Poland, Hungary, Czechoslovakia, East Germany, and Yugoslavia all have fledgling environmental movements, driven to action by some of the world's most polluted conditions.[14]

In Armenia and the Baltic states, environmental issues rank high among the local grievances that have sparked confrontations with Moscow. In February 1988, thousands of Armenians, tired of bearing the brunt of pollution from the scores of local chemical facilities, demanded cancellation of a planned new plant near their capital city, Yerevan. Eight months later, 50,000 Latvians, Estonians, and Lithuanians linked arms in a human chain stretching 150 kilometers along the shore of the severely polluted Baltic Sea to protest Soviet planners' blatant disregard for the ecology of their homeland.[15]

Though the pace of change is slower in Eastern Europe, there has been a notable awakening there as well. Since 1980, Poland, a land ravaged by coal-fired heavy industry, has seen the flowering of at least 62 independent environmental groups—some estimates range as high as 2,000. Their concerns focus on air and water pollution and on the forest destruction caused by acid rain and air pollution. In East Germany, where the winds of *glasnost* are yet to be felt, members of the semi-legal Network ARCHE spread their message without words. By hanging bed sheets from rooftops, they graphically show their compatriots what acid rain does to the earth: the sheets disintegrate in the rain, leaving only tattered strips of cloth.[16]

In those regions where nuclear power is still on a growth course—Japan, France, and Eastern Europe—anti-nuclear movements have grown dramatically since the 1986 explosion at Chernobyl. Intense popular opposition seems to follow nuclear power wherever it goes. In the Soviet Union, public protests have led to plans to close one operating nuclear reactor and to cancellation of at least five planned plants. In Japan, an unprecedented groundswell—the first nationwide movement on an environmental issue in the country's history—has enrolled tens of thousands of citizens with no past experience in political activism. Women in particular are joining in large numbers, apparently sensitized by fears of radioactive food imported from Europe after Chernobyl.[17]

In western industrial nations, where governments place little restraint on grassroots action, community-based organizations set their sights on everything from local waste recycling to international trade and debt issues. In Austria and West Germany, the "citizen initiative" community movement that began in the sixties has gradually expanded its focus from strictly local issues such as school curriculum and traffic control to national issues such as nuclear energy and *Waldsterben*, pollution-caused "forest death." The ascent of the German Green Party in the early eighties was partly a product of this evolution from local to national concerns. The Greens in turn have become the nexus of community organizing across the nation, hastening the spread of citizen initiatives to hundreds of communities. Inspired by their German counterpart, Green parties have sprung up in 16 European countries and already hold parliamentary seats in half of them. Most recently, in October 1988, the Swedish Greens became the first new party to enter the parliament in 70 years.[18]

"Intense popular opposition seems to follow nuclear power wherever it goes."

Until 1986, Italy was among the few Western European countries without a significant environmental movement. A confluence of events, however, has produced a sudden and unexpected outburst of grassroots action. First came Chernobyl, which catapulted Italian Greens into the parliament. Once there, they collaborated with a "Green archipelago" of thousands of community-based groups to call for a plebiscite on nuclear energy. In November 1987, Italians went to the polls and in effect ended the nation's nascent nuclear program. Then, in the summer of 1988, pollution of the Adriatic Sea left Italian beaches littered with dead fish, and toxic waste scandals erupted across the country. Furious citizens, expressing what they called "the rage of the poisoned," staged marches, protests, and general strikes up and down the peninsula. In the port of Manfredonia, where hazardous wastes were to be unloaded at a state-owned agrochemical plant, residents sealed off the town for three days by blocking entrance roads.[19]

Paralleling a steady rise in neighborhood organizing on local social and economic issues, the U.S. environmental movement experienced a marked grassroots expansion in the early eighties. Local concern focuses particularly on toxic waste management, groundwater protection, and solid waste disposal. This "new populism" is the product of forces from both top and bottom: increasing decentralization of authority to states and localities during the eighties and the sense of political empowerment millions of citizens gained during the sixties and seventies. Estimates of nationwide participation range into the tens of millions.[20]

Issue-oriented environmental activism is not peculiar to industrial lands. Just as grassroots self-help movements have spread through the slums and countrysides of many developing nations, so have vocal advocates for environmental protection emerged in most capital cities. Malaysia, India, Brazil, Argentina, Kenya, Mexico, Indonesia, Ecuador, Thailand, and other developing countries have all given birth to activist groups—largely since 1980. Sri Lanka alone has a congress of environmental groups with 100 members. Drawing their base of support from urban educated classes, these organizations form links with grassroots self-help movements and varied international actors such as the World Wide Fund for Nature, Friends of the Earth, and the Pesticide Action Network.[21]

As deterioration of the resource base pushes environmental issues to the fore of many communities' concerns, the foundations of a new international environmental movement are in place. Local and national groups are extending tentative feelers around the world, establishing working relationships on issues of common interest. In the last two years, groups in Africa, Latin America, and Eastern Europe have formed environmental networks that cross national borders, complementing those networks already existing in almost every other region of the world. New continental and global alliances coalesce each year, adding strands to the thickening web.[22]

Environmental movements and grassroots development movements have also begun to interlock. While Third World self-help movements fit a different mold of activism than the environmental movements of industrial countries, the two share root objectives: stewardship of resources, protection of human health, and improvement of living standards for the disadvantaged. Peasant unions know the dangers of pesticide misuse, and urban environmentalists are learning the all-important lesson that privation and environmental decline form a vicious circle. In Costa Rica, at the 1988 General Assembly of the world's largest federation of environmental groups, the International Union for the Conservation of Nature and Natural Resources (IUCN), human needs became the unofficial theme of the proceedings. IUCN President M.S. Swaminathan told the delegates: "A better environment for the bottom billion can be achieved only if we integrate in environmental planning the goals of sustainable nutrition and livelihood security for all."[23]

Over the long run, the bonds between local groups struggling against poverty and groups struggling to safeguard natural resources are likely to grow stronger. More organizations will come to terms with the fact that the environment can suffer because people have too much or because they have too little. And more people will understand that the interdependence of the earth's life support systems turns local problems into global ones. As British Commonwealth General Secretary Shridath Ramphal writes, "Neither the excesses of wealth nor the excesses of poverty can be quarantined."[24]

The Genesis of Local Action

No roads enter the tangle of canyons south of Oaxaca, Mexico, where the Zapotec Indians eke a meager existence out of parched soils. National development efforts, like the roads, have passed them by, but development itself has not. In 1983, a Zapotec youth named Eucario Angeles returned home from university and began talking with people in the communities. What were their problems? What were their priorities? Over the weeks of discussion among local residents a consensus emerged: they should dig ponds at the springs to store their scarce water supply.[25]

Residents assembled two work parties, which quickly excavated two rudimentary ponds. Then one thing followed another. A few minnows whimsically thrown in a pool unexpectedly multiplied, which reminded someone that a visitor had once said something about farming fish. Eucario went to town to find out what he could, and tracked down the Secretariat of Fisheries. There, aquaculture experts supplied him with elaborate specifications for regulation ponds but advised that uneducated Indians would never succeed.[26]

Undaunted, Zapotec work parties set to digging. Despite geologic conditions that quickly ruled out the standardized government design, the workers managed to construct an odd assortment of irregular pools. A year later, tired of waiting for a government inspector to bring them the promised fingerlings, Eucario went again to the city, where he convinced the secretariat to bend the rules and give him a plastic bag containing 175 young tilapia and carp.[27]

By June 1987, when American anthropologist Mac Chapin visited, there were 20 ponds brimming with fish, water supplies were secure year round, and the risk of crop losses had been reduced with irrigation water conducted through garden hoses. Most impressive, the Zapotecs had organized intricate rotating work schedules for feeding the fish, maintaining the ponds, regulating water flow rates, and harvesting a sustainable yield.[28]

This thumbnail sketch of fish farming in the drylands of Mexico is a microcosm of grassroots development at its best. A committed organizer arrives on the scene unburdened with project blueprints or development budgets and begins a discussion to activate latent talents. As community members discover their strengths, they mobilize local knowledge, labor, and materials to address the needs they have defined. From day one, the community controls the process.

Unfortunately, success is rarely as easy as it was for the Zapotecs. Poverty is an economic condition, but its effects ripple deep into the human psyche, devastating self-confidence and self-respect. One consequence, sociologists have learned, is that organizing the dispossessed is much more difficult than organizing the fortunate. Indeed, despite all the activist priests and Gandhian workers, the poor remain the least organized of the world's people. This grassroots inertia is a critical obstacle to progress against hunger, poverty, and environmental decline.

For those who live on the brink of starvation, generations of misfortune and injustice have bred an often overwhelming fatalism. As Zimbabwean organizer Sithembiso Nyoni argues, Third World people are not at the dawn of their history. Life experience counsels them that change is impossible and that to struggle for change is to incite repression. They have little experience, in the words of rural health specialist David Drucker, "of anyone coming from outside other than to further their own interests, to exploit and often to plunder." Sadly, in many countries, this fatalism is still justified. The arms of the state work harder at controlling poor people than at helping them, making grassroots self-help difficult. Where governments tolerate community action, fatalism persists because it is so deep seated. Perhaps most

"Lumping male farmers with landless women virtually guarantees that the men will reap the bulk of rewards."

important, the poor have little margin for risky experiments. Change must go inch by inch.[29]

If fatalism, state repression, and risk-aversion account for some of the impediments to grassroots action, social structures account for the rest. The poor of the world are not, as industrial-country myth has it, an undifferentiated "peasant mass" or a "sea of need." Social and economic roles are as intricately stratified in Bombay slums as they are in the entire cities of New York or Berlin. Research on a Bangladeshi village of 150 households, for example, revealed 10 distinct social classes. Many communities are further torn apart by personality conflicts and factional frictions.[30]

Releasing the traps of fatalism and division usually requires a catalyzing influence from outside the community—"some experience," in the words of development theorist Albert Hirschman, "dispelling isolation and mutual distrust." Broad-based political upheaval can have this effect, as it has in Zimbabwe or Nicaragua, but more frequently an organizer is involved. Given training and support, organizers are often most effective if they are natural leaders from the area itself. These individuals, who generally do not hold an official position, know community members and their strengths and weaknesses. Eucario Angeles, for example, was a Zapotec himself but had received training in community development.[31]

In India, independent groups find that the most reliable organizers are middle-aged mothers: they have good rapport with villagers, especially other women, but are likely to stay put, while younger people often migrate to cities after completing their training. Another lesson from India is that social stratification can make all-inclusive community bodies counterproductive. Lumping male farmers with landless women virtually guarantees that the men will reap the bulk of rewards. Many government community-development programs—in developing and industrial countries alike—have treated all residents as essentially equal in interests and status, allowing the more powerful to co-opt projects for their own benefit.[32]

Every organizing technique is essentially an attempt to liberate the wealth of creative ideas and resources that all human groups possess. Of the two basic organizing philosophies, the first is action-centered while the second concentrates on consciousness raising. The first, typified by the Zapotec fish farming example, emphasizes producing a tangible product as rapidly as possible. Actions speak louder than words, and joint actions tend to create a sense of camaraderie that propels community efforts forward. The actual project can be anything at all: building a school, painting a church, or leveling a soccer field.

A variant of this first organizing philosophy is that of such appropriate-technology groups as India's Center of Science for Villages and the Philippine Palawan Center for Appropriate Rural Technology. Devendra Kumar of Science for Villages describes the approach well: "Technology can be a tool of rural change, because by introducing one simple device, such as a pulley with ball bearings for hauling water out of a well, rural people begin to see possibilities that they did not see before." People rarely seek relief from hardships they consider inevitable.[33]

The second organizing philosophy is typified by Brazilian educator Paulo Freire's teaching method. Now practiced by independent groups worldwide, Freire's method uses informal teachers who guide illiterate adults through discussions of basic concepts from everyday life—such as "food," "school," and "landlord"—to foster a critical awareness of the predicament of poverty. Similar techniques include street theater, traditional dance and music, and oral history. By promoting a sense of identity and self-worth, these methods of popular education all aim to break what Freire termed the "culture of silence" that traps large classes in powerlessness and vulnerability.[34]

In 1975, the Catholic diocese of Machakos, Kenya, initiated a literacy program that, by 1984, involved some 60,000 participants. According to program coordinator Francis Mulwa, "literacy-class discussions became the springboard to other development," generating ventures in handicrafts, tree planting, primary health care, cooperative farming, soil conservation, savings and credit, and water supply. Albert Hirschman calls this springboard effect "social energy": once a group gets started, projects proliferate and momentum builds. Individuals who have once joined a group, furthermore, become more prone to organize later in life. Thus, the importance of Latin America's Christian Base Communities, for instance, exceeds their actual contribution to community development, since a large share of today's community activists got their start in the church programs.[35]

Sri Lanka's Sarvodaya Shramadana overcomes impediments to grassroots activity by combining the two philosophies outlined above in massive work parties and communal feasts where villages come together to speak, listen, and learn. Shramadana means "gift of labor," and Sarvodaya means "village awakening." By giving their labor, people awaken the talents within their village and set self-development in motion.[36]

Fewer obstacles impede grassroots action among citizens of western industrial countries, yet the genesis of local organizations still generally takes a catalyzing experience to liberate community energy. The tumultuous social movements that many nations experienced in the sixties—the civil rights, anti-war, and women's movements, for example—seem to have had the effect of encouraging grassroots action broadly, including among those not involved or sympathetic with the earlier causes. The new populist movement of the United States and the citizens initiatives of West Germany and Austria are thus indirect descendants of sixties activism. In Eastern European nations, however, grassroots momentum is forestalled by the state. Strict controls wall in community activism, and despite the political opening encouraged by Soviet President Mikhail Gorbachev, local organizations remain on shaky ground.

In the best of circumstances, popular action is difficult. The odds weigh heavily against the poor and powerless, so failure is a normal part of the process. But working together has its own rewards. Indeed, the intangible benefits of local action are as important as the latrines dug or trees planted, for as Chilean novelist Ariel Dorfman so eloquently puts it, "How do you measure the amount of dignity that people accumulate? How do you quantify the disappearance of apathy?"[37]

Meeting Human Needs

In September 1988, World Bank President Barber Conable flew to Berlin with a grave message for the governors of the bank and the International Monetary Fund. "Poverty on today's scale," he announced, "prevents a billion people from having even minimally acceptable standards of living. . . . In sub-Saharan Africa, more than 100 million people—one person in four—do not get enough to eat." Conable's testimony confirms what the world's underclass has sensed for a decade: the ranks of the dispossessed are growing. Rising rates of destitution reflect, moreover, a marked decline in living standards for entire populations in Africa and Latin America. In some industrial countries, meanwhile, the gap between the haves and the have-nots has widened appreciably, leaving the average worker with no more than he or she had two decades ago, despite sustained growth in national economies.[38]

Thus, the world's self-help movements are growing amid increasing desperation. People take action as best they can on many fronts, but more often than not they lose. Although the factors that shape community action are too complex to be condensed into a single recipe for success, experiences from around the world reveal certain grassroots strengths and weaknesses. The most important lesson is that community groups organize to respond, on the one hand, to felt needs or threats and, on the other hand, to *perceived* opportunities. There is, in other words, both a "push" and a "pull" to community action, and neither is sufficient in itself. Depending on local needs and opportunities, communities focus on a variety of areas, most commonly land rights, education, health, income, and protecting natural resources.[39]

Perhaps 500 million people live in the squalor of the Third World's mushrooming squatter colonies, and the number grows by thousands daily. In the close quarters of these urban slums, neighborhood associations form readily; São Paulo alone has 1,300. In some cases, they accomplish phenomenal things, as the stories of Santa Marta and Villa El Salvador show. Santa Marta is a vertical labyrinth of houses clinging precariously to a slope above Rio de Janeiro's city council offices. The shantytown is home to 11,500 of Rio's 2 million squatters. Santa Marta's local organization came together originally with the simple goal of starting an informal day care program. By June 1988, however, the group had achieved far greater things. Elected local leaders showed the author dozens of things that the accumulated social energy had brought into the slum: water lines, paved stairways (in lieu of roads), electricity, health clinics, a superb day care facility, and drainage systems to prevent mud slides, which had wiped out two dozen homes four months earlier.[40]

Another success story in self-help community building is Lima's Villa El Salvador, where citizens have planted a half-million trees, built 26 schools, 150 day care centers, and 300 community kitchens, and trained hundreds of door-to-door health workers. Despite the extreme poverty of the town's inhabitants and a population that has shot up to 300,000, illiteracy has fallen to 3 percent—one of the lowest rates in Latin America—and infant mortality is 40 percent below the national average. The ingredients of success have been a vast network of women's groups and the neighborhood association's democratic administrative structure, which extends down to representatives on each block.[41]

Sadly, it is rare for a shantytown to match the achievements of a Santa Marta or Villa El Salvador. Indeed, most squatters have their hands full simply staying put, because fending off expulsion is often extremely dangerous. In Manila's Tondo slum, one of Asia's largest, residents had to form massive human barricades in the late sixties to halt government bulldozers sent to demolish their homes. Unorganized squatters can be driven off at night by police or gun-toting landowners, but organized groups can more often stand down thugs, mount legal challenges, or gain political support. Nonetheless, the land tenure struggle is frequently protracted: the 40,000 inhabitants of Klong Toey in Bangkok, Thailand, for example, prevailed only after a three-decade legal and political campaign.[42]

On the Indian subcontinent, securing land rights is complicated by the rule of slum lords. Breaking their grip requires organizing. In 1980, block committees and an outside development organizer in Orangi, Pakistan, the largest of Karachi's squatter settlements, mobilized people to build sewers. In the process, they managed to shift the balance of power in local government away from slum bosses. Likewise, in 1970, the residents of Ganeshnagar, in the Indian city of Poona, stood down ruthless landlords whose hired gangs were extracting high protection fees. Since that time, Ganeshnagar has been converted into a secure neighborhood with full water, sewerage, and transportation infrastructure.[43]

If squatters secure even limited tenure, they generally proceed to other priorities; prominent among these is building schools for the children. In rural Latin America, it is said that only the church building comes before the community school. Unfortunately, constructing a rudimentary classroom is far simpler than recruiting and paying a teacher.

In Recife, the metropolis of Brazil's impoverished northeast region, 2.5 million people live in shantytowns where barely half the population can read. Two out of three students do not finish elementary school, yet the state government has not responded. Taking matters into their own hands, 60 of Recife's *favelas*—the local word for "slum"—have completed the mammoth organizational task of opening their own elementary schools. These schools, moreover, are not shallow imitations of the tradition-bound public ones: community workers proudly point out that the teachers are local youths and that lessons are drawn from the rich blend of traditional Brazilian and African dance, music, and art that forms the heritage of Recife's poor.[44]

"Our culture had been taken from us—traded for rock music and Coca-Cola—but in the schools we took it back," says Lucia de Prazeres, a local school director. "We discovered that reclaiming our cul-

"**Unorganized squatters can be driven off at night by police or gun-toting landowners.**"

ture gave us back our identity and gave us back our dignity. Learning is impossible if you don't believe in yourself." By mid-1988, the popular school movement was advancing across Brazil. Rio de Janeiro, Belém, and Salvador each had over a dozen community schools, and the *favelas* of São Luis had already opened 40 schools.[45]

Like education, clean drinking water is a high priority for many communities. At least 1.5 billion people worldwide still lack potable water. This leaves them vulnerable to the water-borne germs that cause diarrhea, which alone takes the lives of 5 million children every year. The United Nations Children's Fund (UNICEF) estimates that unclean water combined with inadequate sanitation causes 75 percent of all disease in developing countries. Hundreds of communities are bucking the odds of government complacence and international neglect to meet the need for clean water.[46]

In Dhandhuka, on the barren coastal plane of India's Gujarat state, a generation of excessive fuelwood gathering and overgrazing has led to desertification, which in turn has triggered social and economic disintegration. As cattle died of thirst, the land lost the manure supply and the children lost their milk, making them easy victims for the diseases that prey on the malnourished. Conflicts erupted over water that seeped into brackish wells, and in the worst years four-fifths of the population had to migrate to survive.[47]

As in much of the world, fetching water in Dhandhuka is women's work. Thus it was the women who decided, upon talking with community organizers in 1981, to construct a permanent reservoir to trap the seasonal rains. In this case, an idea from migrant laborers provided the pull that complemented the push of water scarcity. The migrants described irrigation channels lined with plastic sheets, and the villagers reasoned that a reservoir could be sealed the same way. After lengthy discussion and debate, the community agreed to the plan, and in 1986, all but a few stayed home during the dry season to get the job done. Moving thousands of tons of earth by hand, they finished the pool before the rains returned. The next dry season they were well-supplied, which inspired neighboring villages to plan their own reservoirs.[48]

As with innumerable areas of human endeavor, the technical aspects of water supply pale in comparison with institutional and social questions. In Haiti, where less than a quarter of the population has ready access to potable water, the remote town of Coridon spent a decade badgering the government for plastic pipe to bring water from a mountain spring. Then, when UNICEF provided the tubing, and Coridon residents cooperatively ran it up the mountainside, a community neighboring the spring claimed the water, causing another long delay as the two towns hammered out an agreement.[49]

Food scarcity, like water scarcity, may be tackled by community groups. The size of Peru's international debt can be measured in the height of Lima's children: malnutrition now stunts the growth of one in four. Mothers in the belt of hardscrabble shantytowns that encircles Lima have found an innovative way to combat hunger. In more than 1,500 community kitchens, they buy in bulk to cut costs and rotate cooking duties to save time. The kitchens improve nutrition for all while building solidarity among women, long subordinated in the machismo of Latin culture.[50]

As these examples show, community groups are fairly good at confronting sources of disease with an identifiable cause, such as contaminated water or malnutrition. On their own, however, they are unaware of other low-cost preventive techniques that public health experts believe could save millions of lives in the Third World each year, such as oral rehydration for diarrhea, extended breast-feeding, and mother and child immunization. The push of illness is there, but there is no pull of perceived opportunities. Most campaigns that promote these measures, therefore, are initiated by independent health groups or governments.[51]

Nevertheless, such large-scale programs usually make use of community health workers, who need the support of local groups to be effective. Millions of community health workers have been trained since 1980; China alone had 1 million "barefoot doctors" and 4 million health aides in 1981. In Bangladesh, where 250,000 children die each year from diarrhea, the nongovernmental Bangladesh Rural Advancement Committee has gone door-to-door to teach 9 million mothers the use of diarrhea rehydration fluids made from sugar, water, and salt.[52]

Most grassroots groups around the world also neglect family planning, because they lack knowledge of the opportunities or because of cultural opposition to birth control. Spreading the word about the benefits of contraception, therefore, generally falls to a class of specialized government bodies and independent family planning agencies. Where family planning has effectively turned the tide on excessive population growth, however, it has done so through collaboration between local and central institutions. Thousands of mothers clubs in Indonesia and South Korea are the foot soldiers of those countries' highly effective family planning campaigns. In Thailand, the Population and Community Development Association has trained representatives in one-third of the country's estimated 48,000 villages.[53]

Community groups' indirect contribution to family planning, moreover, is substantial. Data from around the world show that as female education, health, employment, and legal rights improve, birth rates decline. Large families are frequently a sign of the subordination of women. Thus, although community groups have had a small role in distributing contraceptives and family planning information, they play what is in many ways a more fundamental role: liberating women.[54]

Through the weekly meetings of mothers clubs, church groups, health committees, and cooperatives, women emerge from the isolation of home and field to try their voices. Gradually demystifying age-old taboos against discussing mistreatment at the hands of men and sexuality, women gain perspective on the hardships of their lives. Growing women's movements in Kenya and Nigeria—where birth rates have remained high since the sixties—may presage falling fertility in the nineties. Since the eighties began, rural Brazil has also seen explosive growth in women's groups, many of them anxious to better inform themselves of their legal, economic, and reproductive rights.[55]

Out of the diversity of community efforts to meet human needs, two lessons emerge: First, local groups are fierce defenders of things they have, such as land for housing, but are less good at getting things they lack, such as water. Second, long-term management, such as running schools, is a greater challenge for grassroots organizations than one-time projects, such as building schools. These generalizations about strengths and weaknesses, however, do not translate into conclusions about importance. Indeed, the most successful communities, such as Santa Marta and Villa El Salvador, are those that strive to gain what they lack and that solve the problem of managing an ongoing endeavor.

Earning Our Daily Bread

Grassroots efforts fail perhaps more frequently in the area of economic development than in the social development areas of health and education. This is not surprising, considering the overwhelming global economic forces constraining the Third World. The causes of poverty in the eighties are many. They include, among other things: a world economy encumbered by high interest rates and colossal debt burdens, heightened protectionism, plummeting prices for the commodities that developing nations export, excessive population growth, resource depletion, environmental degradation, governments unwilling to implement controversial policies such as land redistribution, and national economies that are too restricted to create—or too unrestricted to distribute—wealth. Many Third World countries have seen per capita income drop more during the eighties than did the United States during the Great Depression.[56]

The basic unit of community economic development is often the cooperative, an association of worker-owners who form a business and manage it jointly. Unfortunately, the majority of worker cooperatives survive only a few years. Their members are generally inexperienced in managing capital and equipment, they tend to get locked in a cycle of infighting, and they often face volatile markets, skyrocketing inflation, and policies unsupportive of small producers.[57]

There are striking exceptions to the rule. Bolivia's cacao-growing El Ceibo, Mexico's collective *ejido* farms of Yaqui and Mayo, and India's sugar cooperatives in Maharashtra have all proved that in the right circumstances, workplace democracy and productivity go hand in hand. In industrial countries, where members are often better educated, cooperative businesses often thrive. Spain's Mondragon cooperatives employ 20,000 workers in a wide variety of successful enterprises, and overall half a million Western Europeans are members of worker cooperatives.[58]

Nevertheless, most cooperatives that are based on the collective production model fail because they dilute the incentives for hard work and efficiency. Success is more common in groups that join forces to carry out limited but clearly beneficial tasks. A striking example of this comes from the extreme north of Pakistan, where 800,000 peasants live in one of the earth's most rugged terrains. In 1982, the nongovernmental Aga Khan Rural Support Program began resuscitating the tradition of local self-help through a partnership arrangement.[59]

At thousands of mass meetings, Aga Khan organizers offered support and assistance if the village would form an organization, begin a savings scheme, and select priority projects. By the end of 1987, some 764 of the 1,280 villages had battled their way through daylong meetings to qualify. Villagers have cleared new farmland, boring irrigation lines through mountains and suspending pipes across intervening chasms. They have saved 34 million rupees ($1.9 million), enough to start a regional village bank, and have sharpened their skills in everything from poultry production to accounting. Meanwhile, dozens of women's groups have sprung up parallel to the male-dominated village organizations.[60]

Similar experiences have been recorded around the world. In Taiwan and South Korea, small-farmer associations that facilitate the flow of information and improved seed have been the foundation of agricultural productivity for over a generation. In Zimbabwe, maize production on black farmers' land increased from 514,000 tons in 1978 to 1,780,000 tons in 1985, partially as a consequence of the services provided by small-farmer groups, which grew dramatically during that period. Case studies from Sri Lanka, India, and the Philippines demonstrate the critical role of peasant associations in managing irrigation systems.[61]

In parts of the world, agricultural production and the alleviation of poverty are hobbled by skewed patterns of resource ownership. In agrarian societies, where wealth is measured primarily in arable hectares, to be a farmer without land is to be cast among the poorest people on earth. Where governments are unlikely to meet their demands, landless peasants have little choice but to claim idle plots for themselves.

The Bhoomi Sena land movement of *adivasis* (tribal people) in Maharashtra, India, for instance, has struggled for 15 years to take back its tribal land base from the moneylenders and timber barons who appropriated it early this century. In the Philippines and El Salvador, maldistribution of farmland fuels grassroots action in its most violent form—civil war. And in Brazil, where gross inequality in land tenure hamstrings agricultural production, 10 million landless and marginal peasants began mass occupations of unused private estates in the early eighties and have, in turn, suffered fierce reprisals from landowners. Amnesty International reports that 1,000 Brazilian peasants have been killed since 1980, mostly by hired guns.[62]

For the poor, economic prospects in the cities are little better than in the countryside. Since most of the Third World's urban poor are involved in what development specialists call the "informal sector"—buying, trading, and selling the litter of goods that flow through the world's cities—that is where most urban grassroots economic development efforts are concentrated. Development analyst Judith Tendler

"Where governments are unlikely to meet their demands, landless peasants have little choice but to claim idle plots for themselves."

performed an in-depth review of the economic development initiatives undertaken by independent organizations and found that those most effective at improving the lot of the poor were not the common "integrated" small projects that include credit, management training, equipment, and advice. Rather, success seemed to gravitate to those highly specialized groups that began with a detailed understanding of existing conditions in a narrow sector of the economy. Although grassroots oriented, they were centralized enough to target the specific legal and institutional barriers that perpetuate poverty.[63]

Many of them work primarily with women. The 22,000-strong Self-Employed Women's Association based in Ahmadabad, India, was formed in 1971 as a trade union to fight police harassment and battle for continued access to sidewalk space for street vendors. After each success, they have consciously worked to widen their impact, now extending to female trash collectors and farm laborers. SEWA provides a heartening contrast to most grassroots economic projects for women, which establish crafts, sewing, and weaving cooperatives, activities where markets are usually flooded and profit margins slim.[64]

Many high-impact grassroots economic programs revolve around credit. The Grameen Bank of Bangladesh, for example, has attracted worldwide attention for distributing more than 400,000 tiny loans, averaging $60 apiece. The funds allow borrowers, largely women, to acquire basic capital equipment; they might, for example, purchase a goat, a rice-huller, or tools for wood cutting. On first entering a village, Grameen's "bicycle bankers" simply wander about, chatting with landless peasants about the credit offer. Those interested must find four others and form a "solidarity group" to apply. The neediest two are given loans first, and if they make their weekly payments on time, the other three get theirs; peer pressure takes the place of collateral.[65]

Grameen is not in the business of community organizing, but it has had that effect nonetheless: dozens of loan groups have begun community schools, gardens, and latrines. With more than 100 new branches added each year, Grameen's track record is truly extraordinary and has inspired a bevy of imitators on other continents. As bank President Muhammad Yunus points out, however, short-term credit is no substitute for reforms in national tax, investment, and tenure policies.[66]

Such grassroots initiatives have ameliorated the penury of several million people in the world today, but their impact is swamped by the global economic tide running against the poor. The structure of opportunity in any given nation is determined more by bank credit policies, government land tenure policies, and the impersonal dictates of the international economy than by all the cooperatives, women's unions, and peasant associations poor people can create. Over the long term, grassroots efforts will have to influence these broader forces if they are to do anything more than struggle against the tide.

Protecting the Local Environment

In November 1987, some 2,000 low-caste laborers and farmers from Karnataka, India, performed one of the most peculiar acts of civil disobedience in that nation's history: they uprooted 100 trees planted as part of a massive government reforestation campaign. For villagers to destroy trees in a fuelwood-starved land may seem utterly self-destructive; in fact, it was perfectly rational. The trees were planted by a private rayon company on what had been common land that was open for gathering wood. The poor were simply defending their fuel supply.[67]

As officials in northern and southern capitals alike grow increasingly aware that a healthy resource base is a precondition to real social and economic progress, a stream of self-described "sustainable development" projects has begun to flow from the pens of development planners. Good intentions notwithstanding, this round of ventures could fail as badly as earlier ones if they disregard the lesson of Karnataka. The fundamental questions of sustainable development are, *By whom?*

"Sustainable development imposed from on high is rarely sustainable; it may not even be development."

and *For whom?* Sustainable development imposed from on high is rarely sustainable; it may not even be development.

Environmental quality is not a luxury, as Anil Agarwal of the Center for Science and Environment in New Delhi argues,

> The vast majority of the people of the world—the poor of the Third World—live within a biomass-based subsistence economy. Fundamental needs like food, fuels, building materials, fertilizers, raw materials like bamboos, and various types of grasses for traditional crafts and occupations are all forms of biomass, most of which are collected freely from the immediate environment. For these biomass-dependent people . . . [who] do not benefit much from the gross national product, there is another GNP which is far more important, and this is what I call the Gross Nature Product.[68]

Those who live beyond the borders of the world's industrial economy subsist on nature's surplus—on organic soil fertility for food, on stable hydrological cycles for water, and on forests for fuel. Environmental degradation, consequently, has direct, tangible results: hunger, thirst, and fuel scarcity. No line can be drawn between economic development and environmental protection.

Settled communities generally understand the necessity of protecting the natural resources that sustain them, and over generations, local resource management regimes have evolved. Around the world, many of these ancient systems survive, struggling to maintain the balance between humans and nature. In the flooded pastures along the Niger River of Mali, for example, local and nomadic herders employ elaborate calendars and rotation systems to graze millions of livestock without destroying the land. In the north of Mali, meanwhile, forests have traditionally been managed according to the simple rule that small branches can be cut as fodder for lambs and kids but not for mature animals. Village children provide the eyes of the law, reporting infractions to their elders, who quickly penalize violators by confiscating the best breeding male in their flock. Similar systems are in varying states of health worldwide, from wildlife management in Zaire to soil protection in the Andes.[69]

While historical evidence shows that traditional resource management has never worked perfectly, in modern circumstances three forces have overwhelmed it: governments have undercut local authority, powerful newcomers have put short-term profits before long-term sustainability, and community members themselves have been forced to sacrifice the future to salvage the present when their population surpasses the land's carrying capacity. Communities respond to these challenges with varying success.

Over the course of this century, a procession of new nations, freed at last from colonial bonds, have followed in their colonizers' footsteps by declaring the nation's common resources the exclusive domain of the state. In each case, the same spiral of decline has resulted. When authority over ranges, forests, and fisheries is vested in weak or corrupt ministries in the capital, the tragedy of the commons—in which uncontrolled individual interests undermine the common good—plays itself out in the hinterlands.[70]

Nepal nationalized its forests in 1957, ostensibly "to protect, manage, and improve" them. The consequences were disastrous, however, as villagers' time-honored management systems broke down and the welter of unchecked individual interests overwhelmed government foresters. Twenty years later, the Nepalese government reversed itself, slowly handing over woodlands to intervillage councils. The reform has not decentralized control sufficiently, yet local mechanisms of restraint seem to be recuperating, with dramatic forest restoration in several cases. Unfortunately, communities can do little against this first type of encroachment on their traditional prerogatives. Virtually powerless against edicts of the state, even the best-organized communities generally fail to recapture management rights over local resources.[71]

Communities are both more apt and better able to protect their environment against newcomers who exploit it. These "outsiders" pro-

"The people of the world's disappearing tropical forests, from the Congo to Kalimantan, have begun defending their homes."

vide a visible adversary against which to mobilize, bringing out defense instincts in local groups. Traditional fishers of northeastern Brazil, the Philippines, and the Indian states of Goa and Kerala, for example, are organized to battle commercial trollers and industrial polluters who deplete ocean fisheries. The people of the world's disappearing tropical forests, from the Congo to Kalimantan, have begun defending their homes as well, despite a pace of destruction that makes their task a daunting one.[72]

The world's largest rain forest—and largest concentration of species diversity—envelopes the thousand tributaries of the Amazon River, forming a great fan that covers northern Brazil and spreads into Venezuela, Colombia, Ecuador, Peru, and Bolivia. The traditional inhabitants of this great basin include dozens of tribes of Indians and 300,000 rubber tappers, a guild of workers who trace their roots and their residence in the forests to the cyclical rubber booms of the late nineteenth and early twentieth centuries. They earn their living by tapping the rubber trees spread liberally through the region.[73]

Since the sixties, a series of powerful economic and political forces has thrown waves of landless peasants and wealthy land speculators into the jungles, where they have driven the rubber tappers out—sometimes at gun point. The newcomers proceed to clearcut the woodlands and burn the fallen logs, causing unprecedented destruction and enormous releases of air pollution. In 1987 alone, according to alarming new data from Brazilian satellite imagery, 8 million hectares of virgin forest, an area the size of Austria, went up in smoke.[74]

In the late seventies, a union of 30,000 rubber tappers from the remote Brazilian state of Acre decided to draw the line. "In those times, we didn't know what the 'natural environment' was," Raimundo Mendes de Barros told the author recently. "The forest was simply our life—our survival." At first, their tactics were simple and direct; where the chain saws were working, men, women, and children would peacefully occupy the forest, putting their bodies in the path of destruction. This nonviolent method, reminiscent of Gandhian movements in India, was met with violent reprisals that continue today. Within weeks of the author's visit to Acre in mid-1988, a landlord's hired assassins allegedly gunned down first an allied peasant politician and then a rubber tapper. Then, continuing the cruel history of bloodshed in the rain forest, in December 1988 two gunmen ambushed Francisco Mendes Filho, national leader of the rubber tappers, immediately behind his home, killing him instantly.[75]

The price has been high, but the rubber tappers have made modest gains. Bolstered by an unprecedented alliance with indigenous tribes and the scattered beginnings of a nationwide rubber tappers movement, Acre's union has demanded an end to the destruction of their lands—and an end to violence against their members. They have helped reshape World Bank and Inter-American Development Bank lending policy by showing that, over the long run, natural rubber production is more profitable and creates more employment per hectare than cattle ranching or farming. With help from international environmental groups, the union has called on the Brazilian government to set off large "extractive reserves" where tappers can carry on their way of life in perpetuity. And among the rubber trees of Acre, they have built community schools and health posts.[76]

Across the Pacific, Borneo's Dayak tribe has been less fortunate. The island's dense woodlands are a foundation of Malaysia's foreign-exchange strategy, providing the country with most of its $1-billion annual hardwood trade. The Dayaks, however, want it cut only on a sustainable basis and have battled timber contractors by constructing roadblocks and appealing to European consumers to boycott Malaysian hardwoods. To date, government intransigence has stymied their efforts. The official attitude is summed up by state Minister of the Environment Datuk James Wong, himself a timber tycoon: "There is too much sympathy for the Dayaks. Their swidden lifestyle must be stamped out."[77]

The well-organized Kuna Indians of Panama, on the other hand, have been able to establish their homelands as a biological reserve, putting it off limits to the settlers and cattle ranchers who, predictably, followed a new access road. In 1980, then-President Omar Torrijos de-

"Chipko has gone beyond resource protection to ecological management, restoration, and what members call eco-development."

manded, "Why do you Kuna need so much land? You don't do anything with it. . . . If anyone else so much as cuts down a single tree, you shout and scream." A local leader responded:

> If I go to Panama City and stand in front of a pharmacy and, because I need medicine, pick up a rock and break the window, you would take me away and put me in jail. For me, the forest is my pharmacy. If I have sores on my legs, I go to the forest and get the medicine I need to cure them. The forest is also a great refrigerator. It keeps the food I need fresh. . . . So we Kuna need the forest, and we use it and we take much from it. But we can take what we need without having to destroy everything, as your people do.[78]

The world's most acclaimed community forest movement, Chipko, shows how grassroots action to defend a resource can grow into far more. Born in the Garhwal hills of Uttar Pradesh, India, Chipko first drew fame for its sheer courage. In March 1973, as a timber company headed for the woods above impoverished Gopeshwar village, desperate local men, women, and children rushed ahead of them to *chipko* (literally, "hug" or "cling to") the trees, daring the loggers to let the axes fall on their backs.[79]

Since its initial success, the movement has deepened its ecological understanding and, in the words of movement follower Vandana Shiva, "widened from embracing trees to embracing mountains and waters." In 1987, for example, activists formed a seven-month blockade at a limestone quarry that was recklessly destroying the ecosystem of an entire valley. Chipko has gone beyond resource protection to ecological management, restoration, and what members call "eco-development." The women who first guarded trees from loggers now plant trees, build soil-retention walls, and prepare village forestry plans.[80]

Most of the world's hundreds of local movements for resource protection never draw international attention as has Chipko. A representative case comes from a rudimentary settlement called Zapocó in one of Bolivia's most isolated regions. There, 170 Ayoréode and Chiquitano Indians have built a small sawmill and learned the fundamentals of sustainable forestry in a bid to fend off the commercial timber companies encroaching on their lands. Convoluted Bolivian forest laws—which simply write off the Ayoréodes and Chiquitanos as "savages"—make legally establishing themselves as the timber contractors for the region the only way they can assert control over their forests. Ironically, in this case, a sawmill was the best defense against the chain saw.[81]

Groups organize most readily to defend their resource base against the incursion of outsiders, but in the right circumstances they may organize to reverse deterioration driven by forces internal to the community. Shridath Ramphal writes,

> Poor people often destroy their own environment—not because they are ignorant, but to survive. They over-exploit thin soils, over-graze fragile grasslands, and cut down dwindling forest stocks for firewood. In the context of the short-term needs of an individual, each decision is rational; in a long-term and wider context, the effects are disastrous. . . . Poverty is both a cause and an effect of environmental degradation.[82]

As Kenya's forests shrink, thousands of women's groups, youth clubs, and harambee (let's pull together) societies have mounted local tree planting drives. The National Council of Women of Kenya inaugurated its Greenbelt Movement in 1977, calling on women's groups across the country to turn open spaces, school grounds, and roadsides into forests. Over a million trees in 1,000 greenbelts are now straining skyward, 20,000 mini-greenbelts have taken root, and 670 community tree nurseries are in place. Meanwhile, Kenya's largest women's development network, Maendeleo Ya Wanawake, with its 10,000 member groups, initiated a campaign in 1985 to construct improved, wood-saving cookstoves.[83]

Kenya takes soil conservation as seriously as tree planting, and again women are the mainstay of the crusade. Writer Paul Harrison relates a tale representative of their achievements. Kimakimu hill, which towers over the town of Machakos, was so badly eroded from forest clearing and plowing that gaping chasms had opened on the face. "In 1981, the Kaluodi women's group began an ambitious series of conservation works on the hillside. By 1985 all but a handful of farms were terraced, and the whole hillside was notched with zigzagging cut-off drains to channel rainwater away from the fields."[84]

An African federation popularly known as Naam is among the most successful of the world's grassroots movements at mobilizing people to protect and restore natural resources in an area degraded from overuse. Building on pre-colonial self-help traditions, Naam taps vast stores of peasant knowledge, creativity, and energy to loosen the grip of poverty and ecological deterioration in the drought-prone Sahel. With origins in Burkina Faso, it now spills over under different names into Mauritania, Senegal, Mali, Niger, and Togo.[85]

Each year during the dry season, thousands of Naam villages undertake projects that they choose and design with minimal assistance from outsiders. Along with five neighboring communities, for example, Somiaga built a large dam and a series of check dams to trap drinking and irrigation water and to slow soil erosion. Villagers piled caged rocks by hand to form a dam 4 meters high and 180 meters long. Meanwhile, hundreds of Naam farmers have adopted a simple technique of soil and water conservation developed by Oxfam-UK, in which stones are piled in low rows along the contour to hold back the runoff from torrential rains. While halting soil loss, these *diguetes* increase crop yields dramatically.[86]

The people of wealthy nations do not live in biomass-based economies. Their dependence on natural systems is buffered by the long chains of commerce and industrial production. The industrial economy is too new and too complex to be regulated by traditional practices; its environmental side effects can only be controlled by law. The environmental threats of industrialization that directly impinge on communities, moreover, are not typically resource depletion but pollution. All of these factors make industrial-country community action markedly different from Third World self-help.

Stretching along the banks of the Mississippi River for 85 miles north of New Orleans lies America's "Petrochemical Corridor," producer of one-fifth of the nation's petrochemicals. Hundreds of tons of mutagenic, carcinogenic, and embryotoxic materials leak into the groundwater, are pumped into the river, and spew from rows of smokestacks. The volatile mixture makes the area, in the words of one health specialist, "a massive human experiment." In national cancer registries the region juts out like a red flag, but regulation has been lax.[87]

Neighborhoods up and down the corridor have organized to protect themselves. The predominantly black residents of Revelletown, Louisiana, a two-street clapboard community in the shadows of a mammoth chemical facility, grew alarmed when they began waking up gasping for air. Plant representatives were uncooperative. "No one ever told us what was going on over there," says community activist Janice Dickerson. Local organizers got the 75 residents' blood tested, and found that many of the inhabitants of the community had vinyl chloride—a potent carcinogen and the main product of the chemical plant—coursing through their veins.[88]

The residents brought suit but, faced with the prospect of continuing to live under the smokestacks through years of litigation, most accepted a substantial sum to settle out of court and relocate. Revelletown now stands vacant, while the plant keeps making vinyl chloride and other toxic substances. Dozens of nearby communities, meanwhile, organized a march the length of the corridor to draw attention to the region's plight and to unify their disparate efforts.[89]

The United States has hundreds of Revelletowns which are together forging the basis of a new environmentalism, a movement propelled by working-class communities concerned about local issues. In the Bronx, New York, Patricia Nonnon and her neighbors, alarmed at the high incidence of various diseases, are demanding the cleanup of an abandoned hazardous waste dump. The pesticides that satu-

"The predominantly black residents of Revelletown, Louisiana, grew alarmed when they began waking up gasping for air."

rate the San Joaquin Valley of California take their toll on local children, and mothers such as Connie Rosales of McFarlane Township, where cancer rates among children are eight times the expected incidence, have demanded action from state officials. In Seattle, Washington, plans to construct a waste incinerator ignited such opposition from community groups that the municipal government opted for a city-wide recycling program. Within a year, Seattle was recycling more of its solid waste than any other urban area in the country.[90]

Poland, particularly in the north, can be described in terms similar to the Petrochemical Corridor: nearly half of the nation's water is classified as unfit even for industrial use, and the Polish Academy of Sciences projects that there may be no safe drinking water in Poland by the turn of the century. French scientist Jean Pierre Lasota writes, "According to government reports (many of which are not intended for public distribution), air, water, and soil pollution are so hazardous in Poland that the health of at least one-third of the country's population is at risk: that is, roughly 13 million people now living there are likely to acquire environmentally induced cancers, respiratory diseases, or a host of other illnesses."[91]

The fast-growing Polish environmental movement has not failed to respond. In late 1986, one of the most daring groups, Freedom and Peace (known by its Polish acronym, WiP) mobilized in the city of Wroclaw to demand closure of a steel mill that was endangering their drinking water. After three public protests, two of which were broken up by police, the government decided to shut the plant by 1992. WiP, born out of the Solidarity trade union movement, takes the view that the only answer to Poland's environmental crisis is "for society to organize on the local level to attack the hazards one by one."[92]

The scale of some of the environmental excesses of industrialism makes local responses difficult. Acid rain, for example, undermines whole ecosystems, killing off first fish, then trees. But mobilizing a community against it is challenging, because it is both gradual and may be caused by industries hundreds of miles away. In the United

States, however, the National Audubon Society has found a way to bring the impact of acid rain home. Three hundred volunteers armed with buckets and pH test strips started measuring the acidity of the rain falling on their communities in 1987. The nationwide network draws a great deal of local press attention, and that translates into increased pressure on lawmakers to enact strict acid rain legislation.[93]

Typically, community-based organizations are best at guarding local environments against local sources of environmental decline. Occasionally, as with acid rain monitoring, they work to control distant dangers. Some environmental threats, however, while they have local causes, have consequences that are delayed several decades and are spread around the globe. Indeed, these perils—chiefly depletion of the ozone layer and catastrophic climate change—may come to dominate the decades ahead. Grassroots movements today face the challenge of extending their vision beyond tangible local problems to invisible global ones. Unprecedented dangers call for unprecedented foresight; they also call for new relationships between the grassroots and broader institutions.

Reforming Development Assistance

The paradox of the relationship between Third World community movements and international development institutions is that both subscribe to the same goals and both need what the other has, yet only rarely have they worked together effectively. Despite some recent accommodations on each side, many community organizations continue to have deep misgivings about what they perceive as heavy-handed interventionism on the part of multilateral and bilateral bodies such as the World Bank and the U.S. Agency for International Development (AID). Development agencies, for their part, generally continue to view community organizations as unstable amateurs, junior partners in the serious business of development.

An important distinction untangles the issues that bind foreign assistance—the distinction between aid and development. Much that

"Development assistance per capita to El Salvador is three times that to Bolivia, though Bolivia is a poorer nation by far."

passes as aid does not foster development, while much development has nothing to do with aid. Real development is the process whereby individuals and societies build the capacity to meet their own needs and improve the quality of their own lives. Physically, it means finding solutions to the basic necessities of nutritious food, clean water, adequate clothing and shelter, and access to basic health care. Socially, it means developing the institutions that can promote the public good and restrain individual excess. Individually, it means self-respect, for without personal dignity economic progress is a charade.

Two fundamental and interrelated questions arise in evaluating development assistance: quantity and quality. The U.S. foreign assistance budget for fiscal year 1988 amounted to $14 billion, but subtracting military aid and economic support to strategic countries leaves only $6 billion for development assistance. This remainder is distributed based on criteria more political than humanitarian. Development assistance per capita to El Salvador is three times that to Bolivia, for instance, though Bolivia is a poorer nation by far.[94]

Aid quality is determined by the degree to which development dollars are distributed based on the needs and priorities of the world's poor. Donors' records vary, but few are outstanding. Japanese assistance, which in part because of shifting exchange rates now surpasses American development aid, has traditionally been a slightly disguised form of export promotion, and many nations tie the bulk of their aid to the purchase of equipment produced within their borders. Scandinavian countries' development assistance, while small in absolute terms, sets a high standard for its nonpolitical distribution and its consistent focus on helping the poor. In almost all cases, however, more than half of each aid dollar is spent in the donor nation itself—on machinery, supplies, and salaries for consultants.[95]

Total aid flowing from wealthy to poor nations totaled $49 billion in 1986. (See Table 2.) International charities such as Oxfam and Save the Children contributed $3.3 billion, and the remainder came from national governments directly or through multilateral institutions. The World Bank is the centerpiece of the international assistance system,

Table 2: International Development Assistance, 1986

Source	Quantity (billion dollars)
Western Europe	19.0
United States	9.6
Japan	5.6
Soviet Union, Eastern Europe	4.6
Oil Exporting Nations (OPEC)	4.6
International Charities	3.3
Total[1]	49.2

[1]Includes $2.5 billion from Canada and other sources.

Source: Organization for Economic Cooperation and Development, *Development Cooperation, 1987 Report* (Paris: 1988).

channeling almost $15 billion in fiscal 1988, of which approximately one-third was lent at low interest rates. An ever growing portion of these funds go not to particular projects but to governments in lump sums in exchange for agreements to change domestic economic policies—known as "structural adjustment." The size of international debt payments puts aid figures in context. In 1988, poor nations gave rich nations $43 billion more in interest and principal payments than they received in new loans.[96]

International development institutions began singing the praises of popular participation in the fifties, but real reform has been slow in coming. For most governments and development agencies, "grassroots participation" means asking peasants and slum dwellers to build their own roads and schools—things those same authorities would never dream of demanding that the rich do. Some European agencies and many charitable donors go further toward putting participation into practice, but still, development assistance that is truly responsive to the initiatives of the poor is rare. Oxfam-UK and its namesakes in Belgium, Canada, and the United States are notable exceptions, having been committed to supporting local initiatives for perhaps longer than any other major charitable donor.[97]

This cautionary note notwithstanding, many development assistance institutions do seem to be in the midst of a period of re-evaluation. Decades of a track record that can at best be termed disappointing has prompted them to look for more people-centered approaches. Real progress has been made in the last year at both the World Bank and the United Nations Development Program in establishing the groundwork for collaborating with the grassroots. A growing fraction of bilateral assistance, meanwhile, is already channeled through northern charities such as CARE, seen by development agencies as a cost-effective alternative to weak or corrupt government ministries. This practice could be a mixed blessing, however, if it jeopardizes the charities' greatest advantage—autonomy.[98]

Grassroots development seems to have proved its effectiveness to such an extent that large aid donors want to jump on the bandwagon. The problem is, they may jump on with all their weight, without first undergoing the necessary restructuring and reorientation. They could simply try to enlist grassroots groups as new implementation arms for their own plans, rather than going through the process—often a painfully slow one—of learning to plan projects and policies in consultation with the grassroots groups. The gap between aid and development will close only when aid is made accountable to its intended beneficiaries. Institutionalizing accountability to the poor in development agencies requires allowing, even encouraging, the dispossessed to participate in planning and decision making.

Even when development agencies want to work with the grassroots, it is not easy. The basic problem is an intense clash of organizational cultures between the bureaucracy of aid agencies and what could be called the "visionary ad hoc-racy" of community groups. Operating in the context of destitute villages and slums, local groups confront constant change, unstable priorities, and short-lived opportunities; their working relations are founded not on contractual obligations but on mutual trust. The resulting clash of cultures leaves both sides resentful and discontent. The creative energy and commitment of community workers is wasted filing reports and stifled by arbitrary planning periods. Aid administrators' technical training, meanwhile, is useless in the face of the unpredictability of the grassroots process.

As mentioned above, multilateral development banks pay a growing share of their aid directly into national treasuries to ease the transition to policies aimed at promoting economic growth by attacking inefficiency. These structural adjustment loans, long practiced by the International Monetary Fund but also increasingly by the World Bank, commonly include provisions for currency devaluation, export promotion, privatization of state industries, and drastic reductions in government spending (which generally translates into disproportionate cuts in "soft" budget areas such as health and education). Some of the measures, such as ending state food price controls that discourage peasants from producing surpluses, directly benefit the impoverished, but overall the poor have borne the brunt of structural adjustment.[99]

The development banks could use the same leverage that lets them impose structural adjustments to create an institutional environment supportive of grassroots action. Scores of obstacles to grassroots action are buried in national legal codes and regulatory procedures, and many of them could be taken up in policy-lending negotiations. These include the lack of full legal rights for women and indigenous peoples; insecure legal status for squatters associations, independent development groups, and labor unions; credit rules that exclude those without assets; land titling procedures biased against the illiterate; and development planning procedures that do not allow citizens free access to information. Because policy-based lending experience to date suggests that only a short list of conditions can be included with a single loan, changes in the process of policy formulation might be the top priority. Development donors might, for example, request that grassroots representatives be included in policy discussions between the donor and the government, as the Inter-American Development Bank did in negotiations about a giant development scheme in the Brazilian Amazon.[100]

If participation in policy formulation is to become a reality, however, both grassroots and independent groups will have to do their homework. Many understand local realities well, but do not understand the complexities of things like tax and trade policy. Independent groups, perhaps in federations, could begin forming their own policy research arms to serve as a conduit for the knowledge of the poor, which is often hidden from officials. Development donors could further this process of institution building by hiring local independent groups to monitor and evaluate large development projects and programs.

Most development assistance is given as aid to discrete projects, making reforms in this area crucial. The bulk of this aid comes from bilateral donors, such as AID and the Japanese Overseas Economic Cooperation Fund. Because of the institutional structures of the donors, aid is held accountable primarily to donor country political and commercial interests. Washington, D.C.-based development critics Doug and Steve Hellinger write: "An aid institution that is unshielded from outside influences will organize itself internally to respond to those influences rather than to the intended beneficiaries of the aid." A first priority for reforming project aid, therefore, is to insulate it from such forces. In the case of AID, this could be done by separating true development assistance from military and political aid and vesting it in a streamlined institution that has a clear mandate and considerable autonomy.[101]

In the United States, the government-funded Inter-American Foundation provides a model of such an autonomous development institution. Granting sums generally under $100,000 to grassroots groups and independent development organizations through an experienced field staff, IAF reports to a board of directors rather than to Congress or the White House, and is thus protected from foreign policy priorities. In 1980, Congress created a parallel body called the African Development Foundation, which is just now getting off the ground.

The Swedish International Development Authority is similarly shielded from political pressures so it can concentrate on responding to the needs of its constituency.[102]

Constructing an institutional defense is only half the task of making aid accountable to those it is intended to benefit. The second half is drastically shortening the distance between project funders and poor people. As the Hellingers put it, "It is not difficult to see the absurdity of people thousands of miles away continually shaping new solutions to problems they have never experienced . . . for the purpose of assisting people whom they have never consulted." Bilateral agencies would be better in tune with local needs, opportunities, and institutions if the vast majority of their employees lived among the poor in the Third World, both in capital cities and in remote regions. This step in itself would turn top-down institutions into bottom-up ones and lower costs simultaneously.[103]

Local aid representatives could provide funding, advice, and information to grassroots groups, local governments, and other institutions that proved their capacity and commitment to furthering the interests of the poor. Funding could go either for specific projects or, preferably, for general institutional support. For many development agencies, the concept of development translates in practice into a series of discrete, defined projects: elaborately planned and budgeted undertakings with limited schedules and long lists of prescribed procedural steps. For community groups, by contrast, development is a process that at various points may involve particular efforts such as digging wells or planting trees, but that has neither a beginning nor an end, nor a final evaluation or project document. Shifting emphasis to the support of institutions would better mesh aid with local needs. General support for independent community organizers could promote grassroots organizations in the areas of the world like north Africa where few currently exist.[104]

Two smaller problems also reduce the quality of project aid. Within assistance agencies, administrators are often rewarded for the number of dollars they move across their desks rather than their sensitive

"Bilateral agencies would be better in tune with local needs, opportunities, and institutions if the vast majority of their employees lived among the poor in the Third World."

support of the local process of change. It is no surprise that they choose large, capital-intensive endeavors. Most development projects are, in this sense, "funding-led"; *development*, by contrast, is people-led. Those closest to the process of grassroots development rightfully warn that overfunding can subvert local control, distort community priorities, promote capital-intensive technologies over effective local ones, and fuel jealousy between organizations that should be allies. Conversely, lack of funds for necessary purchases of outside supplies causes the failure of myriad community efforts. If funding matches and grows with an institution's capacity to employ those funds effectively, development will be fostered.[105]

The second problem is the burden of paperwork that paralyzes many agencies. An institutionalized fear of misappropriation and graft creates what one AID employee terms an "ambience of pre-emptive cowardice" in large development organizations. Required to account for every cent distributed and tabulate every benefit delivered, assistance agencies demand reams of accounts and reports, prior approval of all decisions, and elaborate planning that extends to minutiae. A British researcher reports that the quarterly accounts a German agency required of a tiny Bengali independent group "weighed over two kilograms and included . . . a line item and supporting vouchers for the food supplied to the dog that guards the stores."[106]

Ironically, despite the paperwork mountains, useful evaluations of grassroots development experiences—as opposed to government projects—are rare, making learning from the past difficult. Finding fruitful but streamlined ways of evaluating and auditing grassroots organizations is therefore a priority. The case of CEDEAGRO, a committed independent group from the central Bolivian valley of Misque, shows how donors and independent development organizations can learn together. Since 1984, CEDEAGRO has gone through annual participatory self-evaluations with a community-development specialist supported by the Belgian charity SOS Faim. The process takes a week and gives everyone a chance to discuss flaws in the group's work. The specialist then writes a report for the funders and CEDEAGRO summarizing the findings.[107]

Of all development funders, international charities have the greatest flexibility, which gives them the opportunity to show multilateral and bilateral donors the way to carry out truly participatory development. Already, at international conferences, the outlines of a new assistance compact between charities and grassroots groups are beginning to take shape. Under the emerging consensus Third World independent and grassroots groups would shoulder more of the responsibility for direct work, as their industrial-country partners gradually retreat to a funding and support role. Simultaneously, international charities would work harder to educate the public in industrial nations about the reality of life in the developing world and encourage their governments to think of the poor as they debate policies on international debt, finance, trade, and foreign affairs. Charities in the industrial world can be a voice for the planet's poor that the wealthy will hear.[108]

Deep down, working with the grassroots is a philosophical attitude, an allegiance. "Grassroots development is a way of traveling, more than a goal," writes Pierre Pradervand, a French collaborator with Naam. "It means being ready to travel in a mammie wagon *with* people—with all the delays, punctures, breakdowns, and sweat that implies—rather than driving along in one's air conditioned Range Rover with two spare wheels, cool Coke in the icebox, and a fixed timetable."[109]

From the Bottom and the Top

Despite the heartening rise of grassroots action, humanity is losing the struggle for sustainable development. For every peasant league that stanches the hemorrhage of topsoil from a watershed, dozens more fail. For each neighborhood that rallies to replace a planned waste incinerator with a recycling program, scores remain mired in inaction. Spreading today's grassroots mobilization to a larger share of the world's communities is an indispensable step toward putting an end to the global scourges of poverty and environmental degradation. Indeed, while national development in the orthodox model places primacy on accumulating capital and improving technology, sustainable development is built first on the mobilization of people.

All local groups eventually collide with forces they cannot control. Peasant associations cannot enact supportive agricultural policies or build roads to distant markets. Women's groups cannot develop and test modern contraceptive technologies or rewrite bank lending rules. Neighborhood committees cannot implement city-wide recycling programs or give themselves a seat at the table in national energy planning. Thus, perhaps the greatest irony of community action for sustainability is that communities cannot do it alone. Small may be beautiful, but it can also be insignificant.[110]

The prospects for grassroots progress against poverty are further limited in a world economy in which vested interests are deeply entrenched and power is concentrated in a few nations. Tight monetary policies and federal budget deficits in the United States drive up interest rates worldwide, and protectionism in Europe and Japan curtails markets for many Third World exports. The combination of international debt payments and industrial-country trade barriers costs developing nations close to three times what they receive in development assistance each year. Thus reforms at the international level are as important as those in the village.[111]

The largest challenge in reversing global deterioration is to forge an alliance between local groups and national governments. Only governments have the resources and authority to create the conditions for full-scale grassroots mobilization. As grassroots development theorist Sheldon Annis writes: "It may well be that wildflowers grow by themselves. But grassroots organizations do not. They are cultivated, in large measure, by just policies and competent government agencies that do their job."[112]

In the rare cases where national-local alliances have been forged, extraordinary gains have followed. South Korea and China have used village-level organizations to plant enormous expanses of trees, implement national population policies, and boost agricultural production. Zimbabwe has trained over 500 community-selected family planners to improve maternal and child health and control population growth. After the 1979 Nicaraguan revolution, a massive literacy campaign sent 90,000 volunteers into the countryside; in one year, they raised literacy from 50 to 87 percent.[113]

In 1984, Burkina Faso immunized three-fourths of its children against measles, meningitis, and yellow fever in the space of three months. Kenya is waging war on soil erosion, as several thousand women's groups terrace mountainsides with crude shovels and hoes. And during World War II, millions of Soviet, American, Asian, and European civilians recycled materials, conserved energy, and planted victory gardens to boost food production. Today, the threat to global security from environmental degradation merits a similar mobilization.[114]

The mechanisms governments have employed to form these partnerships with grassroots groups vary enormously. In China and South Korea, local organizations are virtually an extension of the state, allowing ready mobilization. In Burkina Faso, the government coordinated the logistics of the immunization campaign linking international agencies to village committees. In Kenya, authorities develop appropriate soil conservation techniques by improving on farmers' traditional methods through a process of consultation. The techniques are disseminated by mobilizing extension officers and local officials to work with Kenya's thousands of women's groups and people's organizations. What seems universal among these cases is that government agencies have treated local groups respectfully and as true partners.

A number of intermediate levels exist between government-grassroots mistrust and full-fledged partnership, and the goal of both sides should be to climb to progressively higher levels. After all, many things can be accomplished short of a wholesale government-grassroots mobilization. No state is monolithic; even in President Ferdinand Marcos's Philippines, the National Irrigation Administration transformed itself into a people-centered institution, cooperating with peasant associations. Such changes are already promoted by grass-

"Unrepresentative elites rule many nations, and all too often they crush popular movements rather than yield their prerogatives."

roots groups and could be supported by multilateral institutions like the World Bank. Indeed, international development agencies might look on their role broadly as building the groundwork for grassroots-government partnerships.[115]

Full-scale community-state alliances can only come about when a motivated and organized populace joins forces with responsive leadership. But herein lies the greatest obstacle to mobilizing for sustainability: few leaders are committed to promoting popular organizations. Because government's first concern is almost always to retain power, independent-minded grassroots movements generally seem more of a threat than an ally. Unrepresentative elites rule many nations and all too often they crush popular movements rather than yield their prerogatives; elsewhere, powerful interests vehemently defend the status quo. Inevitably, self-help will clash with these forces, because like all development, self-help is inherently political: it is the struggle to control the future. Environmental movements, meanwhile, make no bones about the political nature of their methods.

Grassroots-government alliances cannot be formed where governments do not want them. But that does not lessen the importance of grassroots organizations. To the contrary, the best hope for pressing governments to work with local groups is local groups themselves. Indeed, over the long run, community groups could fundamentally alter the world's political landscape. Self-help organizations formed in Philippine slums in the seventies, for example, played an important role in the "people's power" revolution that toppled the Marcos dictatorship in 1986.[116]

The motto of grassroots development that emerged from the seventies was "Give a man a fish and you feed him for a day, teach him to fish and you feed him for a lifetime." That aphorism turned out, however, to be triply flawed. First, *women*—even more than men—were the ones who needed fish; second, the rich controlled the fishing rights; and third, fish stocks were dwindling. Because self-reliant localism cannot tackle the broader issues of resource distribution, legal rights, and ecological decline, many self-help movements have turned increasingly to political struggle, bringing them more into line with industrial-country environmental groups that have long operated by political means.

Where governance is undemocratic, however, political struggle holds the potential to erupt into conflict and confrontation, and to end in repression. In 1987, East German police raided an environmental group's library in an East Berlin church, and the same year, a number of prominent Malaysian environmental and consumer advocates were jailed in a broad crackdown. Human rights organizations are as important to building a sustainable world as are environmental and hunger groups.[117]

At base, grassroots action on poverty and the environment comes down to a question of the rights of people to shape their own destiny. The United Nations–sponsored World Commission on Environment and Development is unequivocal on this question. In the landmark report *Our Common Future* the commissioners write, "The pursuit of sustainable development requires a political system that secures effective citizen participation in decision making," and they outline the components of an approach to governance that promotes citizen action. Enforcing the common interest requires

> greater public participation in the decisions that affect the environment. This is best secured by decentralizing the management of resources upon which local communities depend, and giving these communities an effective say over the use of these resources. It will also require promoting citizens' initiatives, empowering people's organizations, and strengthening local democracy.
>
> Some large-scale projects, however, require participation on a different basis. Public inquiries and hearings on the development and environment impacts can help greatly. . . . Free access to relevant information and the availability of alternative sources of technical expertise can provide an informed basis for public discussion. When the environmental impact of a proposed project is particularly high, public scrutiny of the case should be manda-

tory and wherever feasible, the decision should be subject to prior public approval, perhaps by referendum.[118]

Around the world, community organizations are doing their best to put this participatory vision into practice, and they are simultaneously posing a yet deeper question. In the world's impoverished South it is phrased, "What is development?" In the industrial North it is, "What is progress?" Behind the words, however, is the same profoundly democratic refrain—What kind of society shall our nation be? What kind of lives shall our people lead? What kind of world shall we leave to our children? The rethinking that the world's grassroots movements are doing brings fresh hope: Who, if not these millions of local organizations, can build the institutional foundations and define the guiding values for sustainable societies?

At the grassroots, campaigns are underway on every continent: In the war-ravaged south of Zimbabwe, villagers assemble at dusk to plan the wells and ditches they will dig to combat drought. In a Brazilian *favela*, young doctors work with a team of neighborhood women to teach preventive health care. In a Romanian city, an underground environmental movement gathers data on the pollution that laces their air and water.[119]

Whether these scattered beginnings rise in a global groundswell depends only on how many more individuals commit their creativity and energy to the challenge. The inescapable lesson for each of us is distilled in the words of Angeles Serrano, a grandmother and community activist from Manila's Leveriza slum. "Act, act, act. You can't just watch."[120]

Notes

1. Grain production from U.S. Department of Agriculture, Economic Research Service, *World Grain Harvested Area, Production, and Yield, 1950–87* (unpublished printout), (Washington, D.C.: 1988); child mortality from William Chandler, *Investing in Children,* Worldwatch Paper 64 (Washington, D.C.: Worldwatch Institute, June 1985); other trends detailed in Lester Brown et al., *State of the World 1988* (New York: W.W. Norton & Co., 1988) and *State of the World 1989* (New York: W.W. Norton & Co., 1989).

2. In addition to the particular sources given in these notes, this paper is based on visits to dozens of grassroots development projects in Bolivia and Brazil in mid-1988, as well as previous trips to other parts of Latin America.

3. Estimates of global participation in grassroots movements on poverty and the environment are of necessity highly speculative. One attempt to calculate a rough figure for rural Third World grassroots initiatives came to 100 million: Bertrand Schneider, *The Barefoot Revolution: A Report to the Club of Rome* (London: Intermediate Technologies Publications, 1988). The worldwide figure would be several times higher.

4. Sheldon Annis, "Re-organization at the Grassroots," *Grassroots Development,* Vol. 11, No. 2, 1987; cultural transformation discussed in Richard Critchfield, "Science and the Villager: The Last Sleeper Wakes," *Foreign Affairs,* Fall 1982, and *Villages* (Garden City, New York: Anchor Press/Doubleday, 1981).

5. Independent groups discussed in *World Development* (supplement), Fall 1987; Schneider, *Barefoot Revolution.*

6. Information in Table 1 on Indonesia based on James Tarrant et al., "Natural Resources and Environmental Management in Indonesia: An Overview," U.S. Agency for International Development (AID), Washington, D.C., October 1987; Philippines from Jason DeParle, "The Slum Behind the Sheraton," *Washington Monthly,* December 1987; all other countries in Table 1 are discussed elsewhere in text with citations given.

7. Terry Alliband, *Catalysts of Development: Voluntary Agencies in India* (West Hartford, Connecticut: Kumarian, 1983); Mathew Zachariah, *Revolution Through Reform: A Comparison of Sarvodaya and Conscientization* (New York: Praeger, 1986); Aloysius P. Fernandez, "NGOs in South Asia: People's Participation and Partnership," *World Development* (supplement), Fall 1987; D.L. Sheth, "Grass Roots Initiatives in India," *Development: Seeds of Change,* No. 2, 1984; "Growth of Voluntary Action," *Development Update* (Madison, Wisconsin),

January 1988; Center for Science and Environment, *The State of India's Environment 1984–85, The Second Citizen's Report* (New Delhi: 1985).

8. *ADAB News* (Dhaka, Bangladesh), May/June 1987; Joanna Macy, *Dharma and Development: Religion as Resource in the Sarvodaya Self-help Movement*, rev. ed. (West Hartford, Connecticut: Kumarian, 1985); "Mosquito Control without Pesticides," *Panoscope* (London), October 1987; Denis Goulet, "Development Strategy in Sri Lanka and a People's Alternative," in Donald Attwood et al., eds., *Power and Poverty: Development and Development Projects in the Third World* (Boulder, Colorado: Westview Press, 1988).

9. Annis, "Re-organization at the Grassroots"; Penny Lernoux, *Cry of the People* (New York: Penguin, 1980); Rubem César Fernandes, "Sem fins Lucrativos," *Comunicações do ISER* (Rio de Janeiro), July 1985; Rubem César Fernandes and Leilah Landim, "Um Perfil das ONGs no Brasil," *Comunicações do ISER*, November 1986; Jane Kramer, "Letter from the Elysian Fields," *New Yorker*, March 2, 1987; Sheldon Annis and Peter Hakim, eds., *Direct to the Poor: Grassroots Development in Latin America* (Boulder, Colorado: Lynne Rienner, 1988).

10. Robert Wasserstrom, *Grassroots Development in Latin America & the Caribbean: Oral Histories of Social Change* (New York: Praeger, 1985); Albert Hirschman, *Getting Ahead Collectively: Grassroots Experiences in Latin America* (New York: Pergamon, 1984); Leon Zamosc, *The Agrarian Question and the Peasant Movement in Colombia: Struggles of the National Peasant Association, 1967–1981* (Cambridge: Cambridge University Press, 1986); David Francis, "Colombian Official Develops Innovative Plan to Protect Environment," *Christian Science Monitor*, June 27, 1986; Peter Rosset and John Vandermeer, eds., *Nicaragua: The Unfinished Revolution* (New York: Grove, 1986).

11. Lloyd Timberlake, *Only One Earth: Living for the Future* (New York: Sterling, 1987); Paul Harrison, *The Greening of Africa* (New York: Viking/Penguin, 1987); Barbara Thomas, *Politics, Participation, and Poverty: Development Through Self-help in Kenya* (Boulder, Colorado: Westview Press, 1985); Simon Muchiro, "The Role of African NGOs as a Tool for Change," *Development: Seeds of Change*, No. 4, 1987; Pierre Pradervand, "Self-reliance for Survival in Africa: Peasant Groups Key to Continent's Future," *Christian Science Monitor*, March 9, 1988; "Farmers Helping Themselves," *African Farmer* (Hunger Project, New York), No. 1, 1988.

12. Role of African women from Harrison, *Greening of Africa*; Population Reference Bureau, *World Population Data Sheet 1988* (Washington, D.C.: 1988); women's role in grassroots movements from Peter Wanyande, "Women's

Groups in Participatory Development: Kenya's Development Experience Through the Use of Harambee," *Development: Seeds of Change*, No. 2/3, 1987; Gail Omvedt, *Women in Popular Movements: India and Thailand During the Decade of Women* (Geneva: United Nations Research Institute for Social Development (UNRISD), 1986); Kathryn March and Rachelle Taqqu, *Women's Informal Associations in Developing Countries: Catalysts for Change?* (Boulder, Colorado: Westview Press, 1986); Sally Yudelman, *Hopeful Openings: A Study of Five Women's Development Organizations in Latin America and the Caribbean* (West Hartford, Connecticut: Kumarian, 1987); Zubeida M. Ahmad, "Women's Work and Their Struggle to Organize," *Development: Seeds of Change*, No. 4, 1984.

13. Hilary French, "Industrial Wasteland," *World Watch*, November/December 1988; Helsinki Watch, *From Below: Independent Peace and Environmental Movements in Eastern Europe & The USSR* (New York: 1987).

14. Brian Morton and Joanne Landy, "East European Activists Test Glasnost," *Bulletin of Atomic Scientists*, May 1988; William Echikson, "Dissident Groups Defy Government to Aid Environment," *Los Angeles Times*, January 17, 1988; Helsinki Watch, *From Below*.

15. Martin Sieff, "Soviet Armenia Rips Moscow over Ecology," *Washington Times*, February 24, 1988; "Thousands of Soviet Balts Join Hands to Protest Sea Pollution," Reuters Wire Service, September 3, 1988.

16. Numbers of Polish groups from Mark Selter, "Ecological Siege," *END Journal of European Nuclear Disarmament* (London), October 1988/January 1989; Vladimir Sobell, "The Ecological Crisis in Eastern Europe," *Background Report*, Radio Free Europe/Radio Liberty, Munich, January 20, 1988; East German acid rain action from statement of Alan Gussow, chairman of the board, Friends of the Earth, U.S.A., in "Friends of the Earth Established within the USSR," press release, Washington, D.C., October 17, 1988.

17. Soviet nuclear plant closure from news report, *Morning Edition*, National Public Radio, December 13, 1988; cancellation of planned plants from Paul Quinn-Judge, "Soviets Feel Nuclear Protest Heat," *Christian Science Monitor*, February 4, 1988; Paul Quinn-Judge, "Soviet Writer Challenges Official Line on Chernobyl Disaster," *Christian Science Monitor*, October 5, 1988; Bill Keller, "Public Mistrust Curbs Soviet Nuclear Power Efforts," *New York Times*, October 13, 1988; Kathy Glass, "Organizing Against Nuclear Power in Japan," *Earth Island Journal*, Summer 1988; Keiko Kambara, "Foes of Nuclear Power Make Gains in Japan," *Christian Science Monitor*, July 19, 1988.

18. Horst Mewes, "The Green Party Comes of Age," *Environment,* June 1985; Saral Sarkar, "The Green Movement in West Germany," *Alternatives,* April 1986; Charlene Spretnak and Fritjof Capra, *Green Politics,* rev. ed. (Santa Fe, New Mexico: Bear & Co., 1986); "The Green Party of Sweden" (mimeograph), Green Party, Stockholm, Sweden, 1988.

19. Andrew Rosenbaum, "Italy's Green Party," *Environment,* December 1987; Robert Suro, "Suddenly, Italians Express Anger over Pollution," *New York Times,* November 18, 1988; Andrew Rosenbaum, "Italy's Green Party: On the Road to Success," *Ecologist,* Vol. 18, No. 2, 1988.

20. U.S. environmental movement from Peter Borrelli, "Environmentalism at a Crossroads," *Amicus Journal,* Summer 1987; Will Collette, "Citizens Clearinghouse on Hazardous Wastes," *Environment,* November 1987; New Populism from Robert Fisher, *Let the People Decide: Neighborhood Organizing in America* (Boston: Twayne, 1984); Harry Boyte et al., *Citizen Action and the New American Populism* (Philadelphia: Temple University Press, 1986).

21. Environmental movements in developing countries from numerous organizational newsletters; Nalim Ladduwahetty, editor and founding member, Sri Lankan Environmental Congress, Colombo, Sri Lanka, private communication, February 10, 1988.

22. Spreading networks traced in *NGO Networker* newsletter, World Resources Institute, Washington, D.C., and in *Panoscope,* Panos Institute, London; environmental movement in Africa from Paula Williams, "Evolving Concerns," letter/report to Peter Martin, Institute of Current World Affairs, Hanover, New Hampshire, October 1987; Eastern Europe from Friends of the Earth, "Friends of the Earth Established within USSR."

23. "Making Common Cause: A Statement and Action Plan by U.S.-based Development, Environment, and Population NGOs," World Resources Institute, Washington, D.C., 1985; Borrelli, "Environmentalism at a Crossroads"; Swaminathan quoted in Editorial, *IUCN Bulletin,* January/March 1988.

24. Shridath Ramphal, "Poverty, Wealth, and Inequality," in Panos Institute, *Toward Sustainable Development* (London: 1987).

25. Mac Chapin, Cultural Survival, Inc., Cambridge, Massachusetts, draft trip report and private communication, April 8, 1988.

26. Ibid.

27. Ibid.

28. Ibid.

29. Sithembiso Nyoni, "Indigenous NGOs: Liberation, Self-reliance, and Development," *World Development* (supplement), Fall 1987; David Drucker, "Ask a Silly Question," in David Korten, ed., *Community Management: Asian Experience and Perspectives* (West Hartford, Connecticut: Kumarian, 1986).

30. Bangladesh Rural Advancement Committee, "Household Strategies in Bonkura Village," in Korten, *Community Management*.

31. Hirschman, *Getting Ahead Collectively*.

32. Indian women as organizers from Lori Heise, senior researcher, Worldwatch Institute, private communications with organizers in various regions of India during visit in Fall 1986; Indian government community development experience from Gerrit Huizer, "Harmony vs. Confrontation," *Development: Seeds of Change*, No.2, 1984; AID community development experience from Erik Eckholm, *The Dispossessed of the Earth: Land Reform and Sustainable Development*, Worldwatch Paper 30 (Washington, D.C.: Worldwatch Institute, June 1979); U.S. domestic community development experience from Fisher, *Let the People Decide*.

33. Eileen Belamide, "Building Self-help Groups: The Philippine Experience," *Ideas and Action* (U.N. Food and Agriculture Organization, Rome), November 1986; Devendra Kumar, Center of Science for Villages, Wardha, India, private communication, May 23, 1988.

34. Paulo Freire, *Pedagogy of the Oppressed* (New York: Continuum, 1970); popular education from Patrick Breslin, *Development and Dignity* (Washington, D.C.: Inter-American Foundation (IAF), 1987); Ariel Dorfman, "Bread and Burnt Rice: Culture and Economic Survival in Latin America," *Grassroots Development*, Vol. 7, No. 2, 1984.

35. Francis Mulwa, "Participation of the Grassroots in Rural Development: The Case of the Development Education Programme of the Catholic Diocese of Machakos, Kenya," *Development: Seeds of Change*, No. 2/3, 1987; Albert Hirschman, "The Principle of Conservation and Mutation of Social Energy," in Annis and Hakim, *Direct to the Poor*.

36. Macy, *Dharma and Development.*

37. Dorfman, "Bread and Burnt Rice." 61

38. Barber Conable, president, World Bank, "Address to the Board of Governors," speech, Berlin, September 27, 1988; World Bank, *The World Bank's Support for the Alleviation of Poverty* (Washington, D.C.: 1988); Africa and Latin America from International Labor Organization, *World Labour Report 3* (Geneva: 1987); U.S. distribution of income and standard of living trends from "The Goods on Wages," *New Republic*, October 3, 1988; Thomas Byrne Edsall, "The Return of Inequality," *Atlantic Monthly*, June 1988; *Economic Report of the President, February 1988* (Washington, D.C.: U.S. Government Printing Office, 1988); Gary W. Loveman and Chris Tilly, "Job Creation in the United States," *International Labour Review*, Vol. 127, No. 5, 1988.

39. Incentives to organize discussed in Sheldon Annis, "Can Small-scale Development Be a Large-scale Policy? The Case of Latin America," *World Development* (supplement), Fall 1987.

40. Population of squatter colonies is Worldwatch Institute estimate, based on World Resources Institute and International Institute for Environment and Development, *World Resources 1988–89* (New York: Basic Books, 1988); São Paulo from Céline Sachs, "Mutirão in Brazil, Initiatives for Self-reliance," *Development: Seeds of Change*, No. 4, 1986; Santa Marta from Eliana Athayde, Centro de Defesa Rubião, Rio de Janeiro, Brazil, private communication, June 14, 1988; Gilson Cardoso, president, Associação de Moradores de Santa Marta, Rio de Janeiro, Brazil, private communication, June 15, 1988; author's visit to Santa Marta, June 15, 1988.

41. Timberlake, *Only One Earth*; Bertha Turner, ed., *Building Community: A Third World Case Book* (London: Building Community Books, 1988); Pino Cimò, "Managing Local Food Supplies: Activism in Peru," *Ceres*, September 1987.

42. Julie Fischer, "Creating Communities: Squatter Neighborhood Associations in Latin America," *Grassroots Development*, Vol. 6, No. 1, 1982; Janice Perlman, "Six Misconceptions About Squatter Settlements," *Development: Seeds of Change*, No. 4, 1986; Manila from Walden Bello, "The ZOTO Experience," *Christianity and Crisis*, November 9, 1987; Bangkok from Turner, *Building Community.*

43. Norman Uphoff, *Local Institutional Development: An Analytical Sourcebook with Cases* (West Hartford, Connecticut: Kumarian, 1986); Turner, *Building Community.*

44. Alan Riding, "Brazil's Northeast, Misery Molded by Man and Nature," *New York Times,* May 3, 1988; Valdemar de Oliveira Neto, director-president, Centro Luiz Freire, Olinda, Brazil, private communication, June 21, 1988; Suzana Cavalcanti, co-director, Centro Luiz Freire, Olinda, Brazil, private communication, June 22, 1988; author's visit to community schools, June 22, 1988.

45. Maria Lucia de Prazeres Farias, director, Escola Maria Conceição, Recife, Brazil, private communication, June 22, 1988; Valdemar de Oliveira Neto, director-president, Centro Luiz Freire, Olinda, Brazil, private communication, June 21, 1988.

46. John Briscoe and David de Ferranti, *Water for Rural Communities: Helping People Help Themselves* (Washington, D.C.: World Bank, 1988); United Nations Children's Fund (UNICEF) estimate cited in David Douglas, "Death by Water," *Orion,* Winter 1988.

47. "We Can Solve It: An Alternative by the Community," video by UTTHAN-Mahiti, Development Action Planning Team, Ahmadabad, India, 1987.

48. "We Can Solve It."

49. David Kinley, "Water Flows Downhill in Haiti," *Food Monitor,* Spring 1986.

50. Sandra Huffman et al., "Community Designed Interventions to Prevent Malnutrition in Peru: Community Kitchens and Neighborhood Childcare" (draft), Center to Prevent Childhood Malnutrition, Bethesda, Maryland, May 20, 1988; Alan Riding, "Hunger Spreading in Peru Inflation," *New York Times,* October 30, 1988.

51. UNICEF, *State of the World's Children 1988* (New York: 1988).

52. Marilynn M. Rosenthal, *Health Care in the People's Republic of China: Moving Toward Modernization* (Boulder, Colorado: Westview Press, 1987); Golam Samdani Fakir, "The Role of NGOs in Health and Family Planning in Bangladesh," *ADAB News* (Dhaka, Bangladesh), May/June 1987.

53. South Korea and Indonesia from Bruce Stokes, *Helping Ourselves: Local Solutions to Global Problems* (New York: W.W. Norton & Co., 1981); Thailand from Uphoff, *Local Institutional Development.*

54. Jodi L. Jacobson, *Planning the Global Family*, Worldwatch Paper 80 (Washington, D.C.: Worldwatch Institute, December 1987).

55. Kenya and Nigeria from Harrison, *Greening of Africa*; Brazil from Sonia Correa, SOS Corpo Mulher, Recife, Brazil, private communication, June 21, 1988.

56. Per capita income losses from World Bank, *World Development Report 1988* (New York: Oxford University Press, 1988).

57. Judith Tendler et al., "What to Think about Cooperatives: A Guide from Bolivia," in Annis and Hakim, *Direct to the Poor*; Sheldon Annis, "The Next World Bank? Financing Development from the Bottom Up," *Grassroots Development*, Vol. 11, No. 1, 1987.

58. Kevin Healy, "From Field to Factory: Vertical Integration in Bolivia," *Grassroots Development*, Vol. 11, No. 2, 1987; Kevin Healy, "A Recipe for Sweet Success: Consensus and Self-reliance in the Alto Beni," *Grassroots Development*, Vol. 12, No. 1, 1988; Medea Benjamin and Rebecca Buell, "Coalition of Ejidos Report," manuscript, Institute for Food and Development Policy, San Francisco, California, 1985; Indian cases from D. M. Attwood and B. S. Baviskar, "Why Do Some Co-operatives Work but Not Others?" *Economic and Political Weekly*, June 27, 1987; Jaques and Ruth Kaswan, "The Mondragon Cooperatives—1986, Economic Democracy," The Alternatives Center, Berkeley, California, 1986; Dave Forrest and Andrea Freeman, "Mondragon: Cooperative Successes in Spain," *Seeds* (Decatur, Georgia), August 1986; European worker cooperative membership estimate from European Economic Community, cited in Melinda Tuhus, "Worker Cooperatives: The Creative Job Option," *Rotarian*, January 1988.

59. Shoaib Sultan Khan, general manager, Aga Khan Rural Support Program, "Successful Rural Development in the Mountains of Pakistan," presentation at International Forestry Seminar, AID, Washington, D.C., February 2, 1988; Operations Evaluation Department, *The Aga Khan Rural Support Program in Pakistan: An Interim Evaluation* (Washington, D.C.: World Bank, 1987).

60. Khan, "Successful Rural Development in the Mountains of Pakistan"; Operations Evaluation Department, *Aga Khan Rural Support Program*.

61. Taiwan and South Korea from Uphoff, *Local Institutional Development*; Michael Bratton, "Farmer Organizations and Food Production in Zimbabwe," *World Development*, March 1986; Norman Uphoff, "Activating Community Capacity for Water Management in Sri Lanka," in Korten, *Community Manage-*

ment; Philippines from Benjamin Bagadio and Frances Korten, "Developing Irrigators' Organizations: A Learning Process Approach," in Michael Cernea, ed., *Putting People First: Sociological Variables in Rural Development* (Oxford: Oxford University Press, 1985); India from V. D. Deshpande et al., "Water for People," in Korten, *Community Management*.

62. Bhoomi Sena from Guy Gran, "Learning from Development Success: Some Lessons from Contemporary Case Histories," National Association of Schools of Public Affairs and Administration, September 1983; Anisur Rahman, "Some Dimensions of People's Participation in the Bhoomi Sena Movement," UNRISD, Geneva, 1981; Seth Mydans, "In the Big Manila Land Plan, Steps Are Small," *New York Times*, October 18, 1987; Tom Barry, *Roots of Rebellion: Land & Hunger in Central America* (Boston: South End Press, 1987); Alan Durning, "Brazil's Landless Lose Again," *World Watch*, September/October 1988; Amnesty International, *Brazil: Authorized Violence in Rural Areas* (London: 1988).

63. Judith Tendler, "What Ever Happened to Poverty Alleviation?" Ford Foundation, New York, March 1987.

64. Ibid.; Medea Benjamin, "SEWA: Indian Women Organize," *Seeds*, August 1986; Jennefer Sebstad, *Women and Self-reliance in India: The SEWA Story* (London: Zed, in press).

65. Muhammad Yunus, managing director, Grameen Bank, Bangladesh, speech to 1988 Conference of Society for International Development—Washington Chapter, April 22, 1988.

66. Ibid.; Clyde Farnsworth, "Micro-loans to the World's Poorest," *New York Times*, February 21, 1988; Staff of the Select Committee on Hunger, "Access and Availability of Credit to the Poor in Developing Countries and the United States," U.S. House of Representatives, Washington, D.C., 1988.

67. Paul Kurian, "Commercialisation of Common Property Resources, Kusnur Satyagraha," *Economic and Political Weekly*, January 16, 1988.

68. Anil Agarwal quoted in Sunil K. Roy, "Sustainable Development of Natural Resources in the Third World: The Human Equation," in Douglas Southgate and John Disinger, eds., *Sustainable Resource Development in the Third World* (Boulder and London: Westview Press, 1987).

69. Joshua Bishop, "Indigenous Social Structures, Formal Institutions, and the Management of Renewable Natural Resources in Mali" (draft), Sahelian Department, World Bank, Washington, D.C., August 1988; Board on Science and Technology for International Development (BOSTID), *Proceedings of the Conference on Common Property Resource Management* (Washington, D.C.: National Academy Press, 1986); Robert Wade, "Why Some Indian Villages Cooperate," *Economic and Political Weekly*, April 16, 1988.

70. Tragedy of the commons concept presented in Garret Hardin, "The Tragedy of the Commons," *Science*, Vol. 162, pp. 1243–48, 1968.

71. J. Arnold and Gabriel Campbell, "Collective Management of Hill Forests in Nepal: The Community Forestry Development Project," and Donald Messerschmidt, "People and Resources in Nepal: Customary Resource Management Systems of the Upper Kali Gandaki," both in BOSTID, *Conference on Common Property Resource Management*.

72. Fishers movements from various private communications during author's visit to Brazil, June 1988; "Philippines: 50,000 Strong National Fisherfolk Organization Demands Genuine Aquarian Reform," *IFDA Dossier*, May/June 1988; Sandeep Pendse, "The Struggle of Fisherfolk in Goa," *Development: Seeds of Change*, No. 2, 1984; K.G. Kumar, "Organising Fisherfolk Cooperatives in Kerala," *Economic and Political Weekly*, March 19, 1988; and Center for Science and Environment, *State of India's Environment 1984–85*; rain forest inhabitants from Julie Sloan Denslow and Christine Padoch, *People of the Tropical Rain Forest* (Berkeley, California: University of California Press, 1988).

73. Stephen Schwartzman and Mary Helena Allegretti, "Extractive Production in the Amazon and the Rubber Tappers' Movement," Environmental Defense Fund, Washington, D.C., May 28, 1987.

74. Schwartzman and Allegretti, "Extractive Production in the Amazon"; Stephen Schwartzman, Environmental Defense Fund, Washington, D.C., private communication, April 13, 1988; forest fire data from Alberto Setzer et al., "Relatório de Atividades do Projeto IBDF-INPE 'SEQE'—Ano 1987," Instituto de Pesquisas Espaciais, São Jose dos Campos, Brazil, May 1988.

75. Raimundo Mendes de Barros, Rio Branco, Brazil, private communication, June 23, 1988; private communications with various members and officers of rubber tapper union, Acre, Brazil, June 23–25, 1988; Alan Durning, "Violence in the Brazilian Jungle—A Global Concern," *Christian Science Monitor*, August 23, 1988; Marlise Simons, "Brazilian Who Fought to Protect Amazon Is Killed," *New York Times*, December 24, 1988.

76. Private communications with various members and officers of rubber tapper union, Acre, Brazil, June 23–25, 1988; Mary Helena Allegretti and Stephen

Schwartzman, "Extractive Reserves: A Sustainable Development Alternative for Amazonia," Environmental Defense Fund, Washington, D.C., 1987.

77. Margaret Scott, "Loggers and Locals Fight for the Heart of Borneo," *Far Eastern Economic Review,* April 28, 1988.

78. Quoted in Patrick Breslin and Mac Chapin, "Conservation Kuna-style," in Annis and Hakim, *Direct to the Poor*.

79. Mark Shepard, *Gandhi Today: A Report on Mahatma Gandhi's Successors* (Arcata, California: Simple Productions, 1987).

80. Vandana Shiva, "Fight for Survival in India," *Earth Island Journal,* Spring 1988; "Protecting Doon Valley's Eco-system, Problems and Limitations," *Economic and Political Weekly,* October 10, 1987; Jayanta Bandyopadhyay and Vandana Shiva, "Chipko: Rekindling India's Forest Culture," *Ecologist,* January/February 1987; Shobhita Jain, "Women and People's Ecological Movement: A Case Study of Women's Role in the Chipko Movement in Uttar Pradesh," *Economic and Political Weekly,* October 13, 1984; observations of Lori Heise, senior researcher, Worldwatch Institute, during visit to Chipko eco-development camp, Garhwal, India, Fall 1986.

81. Shelton Davis, "The Ayoréode-Zapocó Communal Sawmill: A Social Forestry Project in Eastern Bolivia," *Grassroots Development,* Vol. 9, No. 2, 1985.

82. Ramphal, "Poverty, Wealth and Inequality."

83. Harrison, *Greening of Africa;* Sandra Postel and Lori Heise, *Reforesting the Earth,* Worldwatch Paper 83 (Washington, D.C.: Worldwatch Institute, April 1988); Elizabeth Obel, "Maendeleo Ya Wanawake Organization," *Panoscope* (London), October 1987.

84. Harrison, *Greening of Africa*.

85. "Naam" is a local traditional term; the federation's acronym is 6S, for Se Servir de la Saison Sèche en Savane et au Sahel (Making Good Use of the Dry Season in the Savannah and Sahel); Harrison, *Greening of Africa*.

86. Ibid.; Bernard Lecomte, *Project Aid: Limitations and Alternatives* (Paris: Organization for Economic Cooperation and Development (OECD), 1986); "Can Outsiders Play a Positive Role in Strengthening Grassroots Movements?" *Food Monitor,* Spring 1986; Peter Wright and Edouard Bonkoungou, "Soil and Water

Conservation as a Starting Point for Rural Forestry: The Oxfam Project in Ouahigouya, Burkina Faso," *Rural Africana,* Fall 1985/Winter 1986.

87. David Maraniss and Michael Weisskopf, "Jobs and Illness in Petrochemical Corridor," *Washington Post,* December 22, 1987; Public Data Access, "Mortality and Toxics along the Mississippi River," Greenpeace U.S.A., Washington, D.C., September 1988.

88. Karen Hirsch, Greenpeace U.S.A., Washington, D.C., private communication, December 7, 1988, and videotapes from Greenpeace U.S.A.

89. March from Darryl Malek-Wiley, "The Great Louisiana Toxic March," *Blueprint for Social Justice* (Loyola University, New Orleans), October 1988.

90. Bronx from Sam Howe Verhovek, "A Bronx Landfill Raises Concern over Disease," *New York Times,* June 27, 1988; San Joaquin from Michael Weisskopf, "Pesticides and Death Amid Plenty," *Washington Post,* August 30, 1988; Seattle from Timothy Egan, "Curbside Pickup and Sludge Forests: Some Cities Make Recycling Work," *New York Times,* October 24, 1988.

91. French, "Industrial Wasteland"; Lasota quoted in Helsinki Watch, *From Below.*

92. Helsinki Watch, *From Below;* WiP member quoted in Jackson Diehl, "Chernobyl Awakens Polish Opposition," *Washington Post,* March 16, 1987.

93. Citizen acid rain monitoring from volunteers and staff of the National Audubon Society, New York, various private communications, November 1988. Also see Alan Durning, "Who'll Test the Rain?" *World Watch,* January/February 1989.

94. U.S. foreign assistance from David Obey and Carol Lancaster, "Funding Foreign Aid," *Foreign Policy,* Summer 1988; El Salvador and Bolivia budgets from unpublished printout, AID, Washington, D.C., 1988.

95. Japanese assistance spending from Don Oberdorfer, "Japan Said to Have Passed U.S. in Aid to Third World," *Washington Post,* May 10, 1988; aid tying from OECD, *Development Cooperation, 1987 Report* (Paris: 1988); Robert Cassen and Associates, *Does Aid Work?* (Oxford: Clarendon, 1986).

96. Aid totals from OECD, *Development Cooperation, 1987 Report;* World Bank, *Annual Report 1988* (Washington, D.C.: 1988); debt payments from Clyde Farnsworth, "Money Loss Grows for Poorer Lands, World Bank Finds," *New York Times*, December 19, 1988.

97. Stephen Hellinger et al., *Aid for Just Development* (Boulder, Colorado: Lynne Rienner, 1988); Kurt Finsterbush and Warren Van Wicklin, "The Contribution of Beneficiary Participation to Development Project Effectiveness," *Public Administration and Development*, 1987; Oxfam from Ben Whitaker, *A Bridge of People* (London: Heinemann, 1983).

98. Aid's record from Cassen, *Does Aid Work?*; World Bank grassroots efforts from World Bank, "Cooperation between NGOs and the World Bank, Progress Report for 1988," (draft), Washington, D.C., October 27, 1988; efforts at United Nations Development Program from various field office draft progress reports, Division for NGOs, United Nations Development Program, New York, December 1988; bilateral efforts from OECD, *Voluntary Aid for Development: The Role of Non-governmental Organisations* (Paris: 1988); Brian Smith, "U.S. and Canadian PVOs as Transnational Development Institutions," in Robert Gorman, ed., *Private Voluntary Organizations as Agents of Development* (Boulder, Colorado: Westview Press, 1984); Hendrik van der Heijden, "The Reconciliation of NGO Autonomy, Program Integrity and Operational Effectiveness with Accountability to Donors," *World Development* (supplement), Fall 1987; Larry Minear, "The Forgotten Human Agenda," *Foreign Policy*, Winter 1988–89.

99. UNICEF, *Adjustment with a Human Face: Protecting the Vulnerable and Promoting Growth* (New York: Oxford University Press, 1988).

100. On using policy lending to target the poor, see Annis, "The Next World Bank?" and "The Shifting Grounds of Poverty Lending at the World Bank," in Richard Feinberg et al., *Between Two Worlds: The World Bank's Next Decade* (New Brunswick, New Jersey: Transaction Books, 1986); Brazilian example from Stewart Hudson, National Wildlife Federation, Washington, D.C., private communication, July 25, 1988.

101. Hellinger et al., *Aid for Just Development*.

102. Breslin, *Development and Dignity*; "The Inter-American Foundation: Report of the Evaluation Group," IAF, Washington, D.C., March 1984; Office of Technology Assessment, U.S. Congress, *Grassroots Development: The African Development Foundation* (Washington, D.C.: U.S. Government Printing Office, 1988); Swedish aid from Hellinger et al., *Aid for Just Development*.

103. Hellinger et al., *Aid for Just Development*. On shortening distance between development and the poor, see Robert Chambers, *Rural Development: Putting the Last First* (Essex: Longman Scientific & Technical, 1983). Other important project aid reform suggestions are outlined in Ralph Smuckler and Robert Berg, *New Challenges, New Opportunities: U.S. Cooperation for International Growth and Development in the 1990s* (East Lansing, Michigan: Michigan State University, 1988) and in Czech Conroy and Miles Litvinoff, eds., *The Greening of Aid: Sustainable Livelihoods in Practice* (London: Earthscan, 1988).

104. Project and institional aid from Cernea, *Putting People First*; Lecomte, *Project Aid*.

105. Problems of overfunding based on numerous private communications in United States and Latin America, especially Kevin Healy, Bolivia representative, Inter-American Foundation, Arlington, Virginia, September 29, 1988; Chambers, *Putting the Last First*.

106. AID comment at "Rethinking U.S. Foreign Assistance," forum held by Society for International Development—Washington Chapter, Washington, D.C., September 16, 1988; Bengali example from Charles Elliott, "Some Aspects of Relations between the North and South in the NGO Sector," *World Development* (supplement), Fall 1987.

107. Author visit to Misque with CEDEAGRO team and evaluator, June 8–9, 1988, and supporting papers from Richard Smith, program director for South America, Oxfam-America, Boston, Massachusetts.

108. On new assistance compact, see Anne Gordon Drabek, "Development Alternatives: The Challenge for NGOs—An Overview of the Issues" and numerous other articles, *World Development* (supplement), Fall 1987.

109. Pierre Pradervand, "Traveling in a Mammie Wagon—or a Range Rover," *Food Monitor*, Spring 1986.

110. Annis, "Can Small-scale Development Be a Large-scale Policy?"

111. Steven Greenhouse, "Third World Tells IMF that Poverty has Increased," *New York Times*, September 29, 1988; international debt payments from World Bank, *World Debt Tables: External Debt of Developing Countries, 1987–88 Edition, Volume I, Analysis and Summary Tables* (Washington, D.C.: 1988); development assistance from OECD, *Development Co-operation, 1987 Report*.

112. Annis, "Can Small-scale Development Become a Large-scale Policy?"

113. Zimbabwe from Jacobson, *Planning the Global Family*, and from Timberlake, *Only One Earth*; Valerie Miller, *Between Struggle and Hope: The Nicaraguan Literacy Crusade* (Boulder, Colorado: Westview Press, 1985).

114. Burkina Faso and Kenya from Harrison, *Greening of Africa*.

115. Philippine National Irrigation Administration from Benjamin Bagadion and Frances Korten, "Developing Irrigators' Organizations: A Learning Process Approach," in Cernea, *Putting People First*; David Korten, "Third Generation NGO Strategies: A Key to People-centered Development," *World Development* (supplement), Fall 1987.

116. Bello, "The ZOTO experience."

117. East Germany from Helsinki Watch, *From Below*; Malaysia from Amnesty International, *Amnesty International Report 1988* (London: Amnesty International Publications, 1988).

118. World Commission on Environment and Development, *Our Common Future* (Oxford: Oxford University Press, 1987).

119. Zimbabwe from Dexter Chavunduka et al., *Khuluma Usenza: The Story of O.R.A.P. in Zimbabwe's Rural Development* (Bulawayo, Zimbabwe: Organization of Rural Associations for Progress, 1985); Brazil from author's visit to Santa Marta, Brazil, June 15, 1988; William Mahoney, "Romania Facing Ecological 'Catastrophe,' Underground Environmental Group Says," *Multinational Environmental Outlook*, November 10, 1988.

120. Quoted in DeParle, "The Slum Behind the Sheraton."

Alan B. Durning is a Senior Researcher at the Worldwatch Institute and coauthor of *State of the World 1988*, *State of the World 1989*, and Worldwatch Paper 82, *Building on Success: The Age of Energy Efficiency*. His research focuses on local initiatives to address global problems. Mr. Durning is a graduate of Oberlin College, where he specialized in philosophy and environmental studies.

THE WORLDWATCH PAPER SERIES

No. of
Copies*

_____ 44. **Rivers of Energy: The Hydropower Potential** by Daniel Deudney.
_____ 47. **Infant Mortality and the Health of Societies** by Kathleen Newland.
_____ 49. **Productivity: The New Economic Context** by Kathleen Newland.
_____ 50. **Space: The High Frontier in Perspective** by Daniel Deudney.
_____ 51. **U.S. and Soviet Agriculture: The Shifting Balance of Power** by Lester R. Brown.
_____ 54. **Promoting Population Stabilization** by Judith Jacobsen.
_____ 57. **Nuclear Power: The Market Test** by Christopher Flavin.
_____ 58. **Air Pollution, Acid Rain, and the Future of Forests** by Sandra Postel.
_____ 59. **Improving World Health: A Least Cost Strategy** by William U. Chandler.
_____ 60. **Soil Erosion: Quiet Crisis in the World Economy** by Lester R. Brown and Edward C. Wolf.
_____ 61. **Electricity's Future: The Shift to Efficiency and Small-Scale Power** by Christopher Flavin.
_____ 62. **Water: Rethinking Management in an Age of Scarcity** by Sandra Postel.
_____ 63. **Energy Productivity: Key to Environmental Protection and Economic Progress** by William U. Chandler.
_____ 64. **Investing in Children** by William U. Chandler.
_____ 65. **Reversing Africa's Decline** by Lester R. Brown and Edward C. Wolf.
_____ 66. **World Oil: Coping With the Dangers of Success** by Christopher Flavin.
_____ 67. **Conserving Water: The Untapped Alternative** by Sandra Postel.
_____ 68. **Banishing Tobacco** by William U. Chandler.
_____ 69. **Decommissioning: Nuclear Power's Missing Link** by Cynthia Pollock.
_____ 70. **Electricity For A Developing World** by Christopher Flavin.
_____ 71. **Altering the Earth's Chemistry: Assessing the Risks** by Sandra Postel.
_____ 72. **The Changing Role of the Market in National Economies** by William U. Chandler.
_____ 73. **Beyond the Green Revolution: New Approaches for Third World Agriculture** by Edward C. Wolf.
_____ 74. **Our Demographically Divided World** by Lester R. Brown and Jodi L. Jacobson.
_____ 75. **Reassessing Nuclear Power: The Fallout From Chernobyl** by Christopher Flavin.
_____ 76. **Mining Urban Wastes: The Potential for Recycling** by Cynthia Pollock.
_____ 77. **The Future of Urbanization: Facing the Ecological and Economic Constraints** by Lester R. Brown and Jodi L. Jacobson.
_____ 78. **On the Brink of Extinction: Conserving The Diversity of Life** by Edward C. Wolf.
_____ 79. **Defusing the Toxics Threat: Controlling Pesticides and Industrial Waste** by Sandra Postel.

*Those Worldwatch Papers not listed are out of print.

_____ 80. **Planning the Global Family** by Jodi L. Jacobson.
_____ 81. **Renewable Energy: Today's Contribution, Tomorrow's Promise** by Cynthia Pollock Shea.
_____ 82. **Building on Success: The Age of Energy Efficiency** by Christopher Flavin and Alan B. Durning.
_____ 83. **Reforesting the Earth** by Sandra Postel and Lori Heise.
_____ 84. **Rethinking the Role of the Automobile** by Michael Renner.
_____ 85. **The Changing World Food Prospect: The Nineties and Beyond** by Lester R. Brown.
_____ 86. **Environmental Refugees: A Yardstick of Habitability** by Jodi L. Jacobson.
_____ 87. **Protecting Life on Earth: Steps to Save the Ozone Layer** by Cynthia Pollock Shea.
_____ 88. **Action at the Grassroots: Fighting Poverty and Environment Decline** by Alan B. Durning.
_____ 89. **National Security: The Economic and Environmental Dimensions** by Michael Renner.
_____ 90. **The Bicycle: Vehicle for a Small Planet** by Marcia Lowe.
_____ 91. **Slowing Global Warming: A Worldwide Strategy** by Christopher Flavin.
_____ 92. **Poverty and the Environment: Reversing the Downward Spiral** by Alan B. Durning.
_____ 93. **Water for Agriculture: Facing the Limits** by Sandra Postel.
_____ 94. **Clearing the Air: A Global Agenda** by Hilary F. French.
_____ 95. **Apartheid's Environmental Toll** by Alan B. Durning.
_____ 96. **Swords Into Plowshares: Converting to a Peace Economy** by Michael Renner.
_____ 97. **The Global Politics of Abortion** by Jodi L. Jacobson.

_____ **Total Copies**

☐ **Single Copy: $4.00**
☐ **Bulk Copies (any combination of titles)**
☐ 2–5: $3.00 each ☐ 6–20: $2.00 each ☐ 21 or more: $1.00 each

☐ **Membership in the Worldwatch Library: $25.00**
Includes the paperback edition of our 250- page "annual physical of the planet," *State of the World 1990,* plus all Worldwatch Papers released during a one-year period

Make check payable to Worldwatch Institute
1776 Massachusetts Avenue, N.W., Washington, D.C. 20036 USA
Enclosed is my check for U.S. $________

____
name

____
address

____
city **state** **zip/country**

WWP